Foreword by
Sir Geoffrey Jellicoe

Philip Cave

Creating japanese Gardens

Aurum Press

First published 1993 by Aurum Press Ltd,
10 Museum Street, London WC1A 1JS
Copyright © 1993 by Philip Cave
Hardiness zone maps copyright © 1988 by Hugh Williams

Title page illustration: A scene from the
fifth scroll of *The Miracles of the Kasuga
Deities* by Takashina Takakane (14th century)

A catalogue record for this book is available from the
British Library.

ISBN 1 85410 212 5

10 9 8 7 6 5 4 3 2 1
1997   1996   1995   1994   1993

Art direction: Andrew Gossett MSTD
Design: Studio Gossett
Typeset in Futura by August Filmsetting, St Helens
Printed in Hong Kong

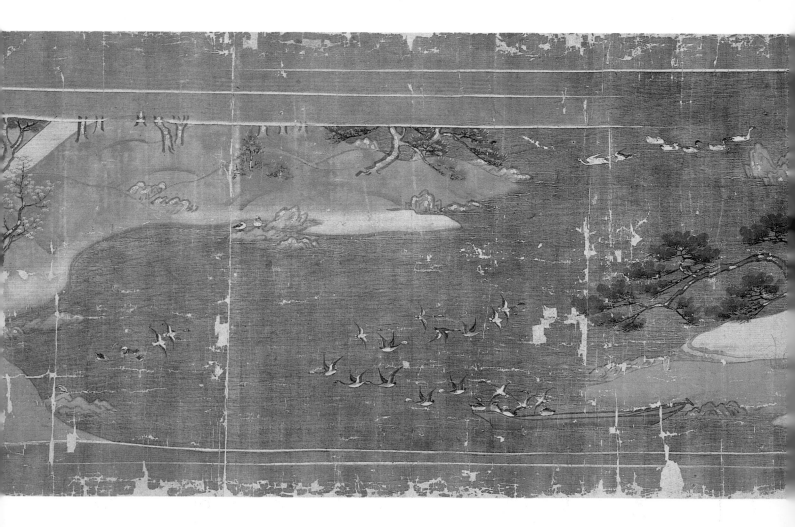

Contents

Sir Geoffrey Jellicoe, CBE, RA is a former President of the Institute of Landscape Architects and Honorary President of the International Federation of Landscape Architects. In 1981 he was awarded the Medal of the American Society of Landscape Architects. He has created gardens for Sandringham, Royal Lodge, the RHS at Wisley and is currently engaged on the *Gardens of Civilization* project in Galveston, Texas, and the landscape of the Atlanta Historical Society, Atlanta, Georgia, USA.

Foreword   Sir Geoffrey Jellicoe

Whether or not you take the Japanese garden lightly or seriously, this book is a very good introduction to a subject that has almost universal appeal. Mr Cave not only presents the historical background with sympathy and understanding but describes the much more difficult task of how such a garden could be constructed in the West. That is excellent, and this introduction can now be directed to the question: why a Japanese garden in the West when our own gardens are in themselves so lovely? Is there some hidden mystique? There is, and to find and reveal it I must take the reader back countless years, before gardens as such existed.

In pre-history the similarity between Western cave art and early Chinese painting (not to mention the burial mounds described by the author) suggests that culture was global before the great split into West and East. Two figures in later recorded history are of profound importance to our subject: the Greek philosopher Heraclitus (*c.* 500 BC) and the Chinese Lao-tzu (*c.* 600 BC), the founder of Taoism.

The Western philosophy of pure reason began with Thales of Miletus, developed with Pythagoras the mathematician, through Heraclitus, to reach its climax in Plato and Aristotle. The primary search, to find permanency in an ever-changing world, was theoretically resolved by the divine geometric proportions of Plato, which became the accepted basis of classicism until the present century. Heraclitus, conceivably the father of modern metaphysics, did not accept the theory of stability, declaring that 'All things are in flux', and would ever be. He probed more deeply into the mind than any philosopher before Jung, declaring that 'The subconscious harmonizes the conscious.' Where Plato set out to dominate nature, Heraclitus would clearly go with it.

The relation of Lao-tzu to Confucius is not unlike that of Heraclitus to Plato, but whereas the Greek voice was smothered until the present century, that of Lao-tzu has been loud and clear throughout the ages, passing in due course to Japan. What *is* Taoism? Loraine Kuck

writes '. . . of hazy unreality that creates in a mind attuned to it the feeling of kinship with nature, the sense of one's spirit merging into the spirit of other natural things and the eternal behind them all'. Yes, but what is the design technique that sublimates these human and natural objects? I suggest it is a hidden sense of movement, one that rotates upon itself and has a certain correspondence with the motions of the cosmos. This sense of self-contained movement is unique among the gardens of the world; without it the charming waters and bridges, the characteristic stepping stones, the symbolic rocks and plants, the stone lamps and Buddhas, would be in spirit like actors on a stage where the curtain never rises.

And, now, why create Japanese gardens in the West?

For centuries Western culture was either classical or romantic, or both. The first rumblings of a new age came in mid-Victorian times and with them the first of the intriguing Japanese gardens, distant country cousins of the rock gardens. Then, at the turn of the century, came a veritable explosion in cultures, and a new age, which could be termed 'cosmic', was born. Throughout the century the arts have been groping for an association with the new cosmic phenomena revealed by science. The Japanese concept of abstract form in flux, originated by Lao-tzu and Heraclitus, is one of the intensely human arts that could make us feel partakers, and not foreigners, in this odd new world of time and space that is upon us.

These words are weighty and should be soon forgotten, for to Westerners the charm of the Japanese garden is that, metaphorically, it is itself weightless. It is lovely to imagine the little Japanese lady in her kimono as part of her garden with its tender scale and apparent informality. Mr Cave's gardens will be delightful to the eye, but even more so to the imagination. Let us remember, too, that we are magicians who never were before, for we can walk twice into the same waters of a river when the philosophers told us we could not. Reader, read on and enjoy.

Preface

The tradition of Japanese gardens has been an inspiration for centuries and yet it is a living tradition, influencing the creation of new gardens and landscapes both in Japan and in the West. Wherever your interests lie – in the theory or the practice, in developing your knowledge and awareness of Japanese garden style or in learning new techniques – this book is intended to help you appreciate and understand this unique tradition. Like any art, all is not revealed in one glance.

There is a growing recognition that a garden or landscape is much more than an assemblage of plants. If you want an area to be functional (a place for sitting, walking, entertaining and viewing), yet at the same time to evoke feelings of delight and well-being, your design needs to be carefully thought out. This is essential whatever the size or state of the garden, whether the area is undeveloped bare ground or whether it already has some sort of a design into which a new composition is to be incorporated. The design must encompass artistic parameters of expression and imagination as well as purely practical considerations.

With these demands in mind, it is natural to search around for inspiration from the great garden traditions of the world – of which Japanese gardens are one example – to study them and extract those aspects that may be of use in creating a modern garden or landscape. Such a study and application should not be confused with mere copying. By developing an understanding of the garden tradition it is possible to create anew with a heightened awareness.

In Japan the distinct style of garden design and construction is a living art, in which old gardens are sensitively restored and new ones are created with a knowledge of the tradition. Although for the last three centuries no particularly distinctive styles have been developed, new gardens have been constructed using age-old techniques and often incorporating traditional symbolic references. Such gardens are not, however, merely copies of older historical gardens; they are new designs, yet are influenced by elements in historical gardens from which derive a sense of continuity with the past and a feeling of stability in the environment. All this has been possible because, until the last century, Japan was relatively isolated and developed within itself. From many of the Japanese arts and crafts practised today an unbroken line going back centuries can be drawn.

A study of Japanese tradition reveals various design principles and techniques that can be usefully and effectively applied to present-day designs in the West. It is quite common for people to try to make a small garden or landscape space seem larger than it really is, but the result is rarely successful. Whereas Western garden traditions offer little inspiration as to how to accomplish such effects, Japanese techniques excel.

The importance of viewpoints, the creation of false perspective, the technique of miniaturization, compositional balance and harmony, and unique applications of rocks and water are just some of the elements of the Japanese style described in this book that will inspire new designs and practices. However, an interest in Japanese garden tradition can be fulfilling in many ways – from the standpoint of garden or landscape design and from the personal angle, as Japanese gardens are closely interrelated with nature, religion and the psychology of the mind.

chapter 1

The Japanese Way

Interest in the gardens of Japan stems from an empathy with their unique qualities: the feeling of stillness and serenity they evoke, their deep symbolic meaning or their developed artistry. They can be perceived and appreciated on many levels, and people find them pleasing or fulfilling for different reasons. One reason for popular modern interest in Japanese gardens is their ability to capture the essence of nature. With more and more people living in cities and towns, the human need for contact with nature is not always satisfied.

Western gardening traditions obviously bring nature into the garden but generally in a humanized condition. The inspiration may initially have been wild nature – for example those landscapes commonly encountered on the Grand Tour of Europe in the seventeenth and eighteenth centuries when the affluent travelled the Alps – but the images brought back, on which gardens became based, were really picturesque and romantic. Wild nature, which Westerners looked on as being apart from them, had to be tamed and organized before it was incorporated in a garden. In contrast, the Chinese and Japanese showed man as being in harmony with nature. Their garden design and landscape painting were interrelated arts, and in paintings man was shown among the mountains and gorges of wild nature, with the overall composition being in perfect balance. They felt at ease with wild elements partly because their philosophy endowed mountains, streams, rocks and plants with symbolic meaning. Far Eastern sensibilities grew out of a belief that man lived more fully by being open to the universal rhythms of nature, becoming at one with trees and stones. In Japanese gardens some of the most prized elements are those rocks that look like towering craggy peaks, or twisted pines that appear weather-beaten, as though they have been on some exposed rocky promontory for decades.

A perfectly composed arrangement at Tenryu-ji, embodying the 'way' in many of its aspects – the waterfall stone at the rear is balanced by the stone bridge in front, the suggestion of flowing water is powerful and the harmony and balance of natural elements here evoke great mystery and strength.

Gardens and Religion

In Japanese gardens there is a recognition that gardens and created landscapes can be more than just a stimulation of the senses of sight, smell and touch. Over the centuries Japanese beliefs and religions have been intimately associated with the arts, of which garden design is one. As these beliefs and religions were concerned with aspects of the universe that were more profound than the senses, so too were the arts of Japan. The belief that natural objects were the abode of spirits came from Shinto, the indigenous religion of Japan, and one result is a firmly implanted reverence for nature in the Japanese people. In later years, Buddhists tried to create a paradise on earth as an example of what can be achieved by religious efforts. This paradise was initially depicted in paintings but was then created as gardens. Subsequently, Zen Buddhism inspired people to design gardens for contemplative or meditative practices, or to illustrate a particular Zen concept. In fact, as garden designers were usually also priests or monks, the garden became a measure of their spiritual insight. Considering this historical relationship with religion, it is no wonder that Japanese gardens can evoke, now as then, a deep resonance.

No garden can be more universal than Ryoan-ji. It uniquely embodies the Zen aesthetic in its most severe form, and silently but forcefully leads the mind and the imagination to contemplate the meaning of the absolute, which is limitless.

15

The tokonoma, or alcove, in a Japanese home provides the
setting for a single perfectly placed object for the purpose
of contemplation or meditation.

Symbolism

For any garden or work of art to affect someone at a level deeper than the immediate senses, the composition needs to trigger a profound psychological and emotional response within that person. It is a fundamental aim of Japanese gardens to do exactly this, through the use of symbols. In order to understand symbolism, we need to look at two authorities on the subject – Gregory Kepes and Carl Jung.

Kepes defined symbols as human creations by which we transform the physical environment around us into meanings and values. Thus, we use symbols to make our surroundings more legible, more comprehensible. It is thought that the unconscious part of our mind stores experiences and associations, and when we travel to unfamiliar surroundings the likeness to familiar associations is recalled, thereby making us feel at ease.

Carl Jung described the psyche as consisting of both the conscious and unconscious mind, the latter being divided into the personal unconscious and the collective unconscious. It is the human collective unconscious that stores its own history, built up over man's previous development, right back to the mind of ancient man. If such a premise is correct, humans must retain an unconscious identification with nature from their evolutionary past. By going out into nature and experiencing certain symbols, we are unknowingly linking ourselves with the vast collective unconscious. In creating these symbols in the context of a garden, this link can again be made.

Whether or not a symbol triggers a certain response depends on the state of mind of the person experiencing it and on the make-up of their unconscious. To someone whose history and current sympathies are in the Zen tradition, the rock and gravel garden at Ryoan-ji (see pp.54–5) is experienced in a particular way. To that person, rocks floating in a sea of gravel might symbolize our microcosm moving in the infinite universe or macrocosm or, indeed, the rocks might symbolize thoughts in a limitless void. The ripples in the gravel around the stone could symbolize the fact that still water (representing the mind) reflects pure reality, but as soon as stone (representing thought) causes a ripple, then reality becomes distorted.

However, to a mind not trained in Zen or similar traditions, it might simply symbolize islands in a sea or mountains above the clouds.

A good example of symbols are objects placed in the *tokonoma* (see opposite). The *tokonoma* is an element of the Japanese house that has no Western equivalent. It developed from a private altar in the house of a Zen Buddhist priest. Here it was a low table, on which were placed such objects as an incense burner and flower vessel, with a Buddhist scroll above. In later years the *tokonoma* developed into an alcove and then became an important focus of the Japanese house, where art objects, such as scroll paintings, flower arrangements or ceramics, are displayed. As there are only one or possibly two objects on show they take on great importance. One flower alone can be a symbol that will link someone to the creativity of nature and, by extension, one tree in a garden is all that is needed to symbolize a wood or, indeed, vast nature itself.

The rock in the shape of a boat at Daisen-in creates in one's mind a river scene, with the boat slowly bobbing up and down on the 'water'.

Previous pages: The temple at Shisen-do opens out on to a stunning garden of carefully clipped bushes. The room and the garden seem as one.

Right: A landscape in Haboku style by the priest-gardener Sesshu Toyo (1420–1506), whose work was filled with Zen symbolism (see p.46).

Developing a Sensitivity

A story about Sen no Rikyu, the great tea master, is a good way to illustrate the kind of sensitivity that needs to be cultivated in order to design and appreciate gardens. The story tells of a stone water basin that stood in a garden near Osaka with a fine view of the Inland Sea. Apparently, Rikyu planted two hedges, one outside the other, in such a way that they completely obscured the beautiful view of the Inland Sea. Only when a guest bent over the water basin to dip for water with his hands could he see the sea in a break between the hedges. Rikyu deliberately designed the garden in this way in the hope that the guest would see his mind reflected in the water in the basin and then, looking up to see the infinite ocean, would realize that the water and the ocean are one, in just the same way that the mind and the infinite are one. This story also shows how elements of surprise and spontaneity can be designed into a garden.

Japanese garden designers began by studying nature in all its various forms — actual physical nature, and nature as depicted by landscape painters. This way they perceived an artist's view of nature, which was important, since in no way could a garden designer impart a natural scene in total. Both the painter and the garden designer tried to experience — and in some way comprehend — the essence of a natural scene, and then bring it in its simplified form, reduced in scale, into the garden. Basically this meant picking up on those elements which seemed to symbolize the natural scene and then forming them into a composition. Hopefully, someone looking at the garden composition would unconsciously cue into the symbol that would link them back to the actual scene.

The symbols created in the garden are not always taken from nature but, in the case of Zen gardens, from the metaphysical. In this case the designer may be attempting

Left: Sketch of a water basin arrangement for a new garden in the traditional style designed by Professor Kinsaku Nakane.

Below: This sea-shore at Harris, in the Outer Hebrides, could provide the inspiration for a garden, through a study of the rock compositions, their relationship to water and to the island beyond.

to connect the viewer to a particular Zen truth, or indeed directly to *satori* (enlightenment). The lotus is a symbol of enlightenment — the roots are embedded in the mud (of human passions), the flower and leaves are open to the sun (and purity). Zen gardens were often abstract and minimal so that the viewer could be taken more directly to the truth.

To cultivate such a sensitivity and awareness one must learn to share the interests of previous garden designers. For example, elements of Chinese culture, such as religion, landscape and painting, were gradually assimilated into Japanese art and culture until they became totally Japanese. Japanese religions, from Shinto to Zen Buddhism, had a great influence on garden designers; and, of course, the tea masters and the tea ceremony had a lasting effect on garden design and on the sensibilities of the Japanese people as a whole. With this newly acquired sensitivity you will perceive historical gardens, and gardens designed now in a traditional style, in a new light. Whether through pictures in books or by actually visiting them in person, you should appreciate Japanese gardens on levels not previously realized.

By going to the source you avoid being a mere copyist of a particular style and simply importing interesting-looking elements without any real understanding of them. Anyone can buy a variety of Japanese garden ornaments and sprinkle them liberally around a garden space, adding a few rocks and bamboo, but the relation to the Japanese tradition will be tenuous. Those who have developed a sensitivity to the Japanese style can take hold of the true spirit of the art and create gardens in sympathy with their own personal traditions, their outlook on life and physical setting.

Climate and Topography

Before commencing any study, some knowledge of the physical setting of historical gardens is needed. Japan is a group of islands of generally mountainous terrain. Numerous water courses begin as tumbling mountain streams, giving way to broad rivers, which become beds of pebbles during dry periods. The Inland Sea, situated between two of the larger islands, is a spectacular sight, with deep scalloped bays and pine-clad headlands that have constantly inspired garden compositions. The temperate climate, abundant rainfall and warm ocean currents have encouraged a heavy growth of forest. Only about 20 per cent of the land can be cultivated and the fields are a mosaic of dykes, which explains the traditional Japanese skill in manipulating water. There is a marked difference between the seasons, with snow in the winter and hot, humid summers. Most of the remaining historical gardens of Japan are in Kyoto, which is particularly humid, making it ideal for the growing of the much-prized moss, which is an important and striking feature of many gardens.

Relationship to Buildings

With the exception of early Shinden-style mansions (see p.34), Japanese buildings and the daily lives of the people who live in them all have a close relationship with the garden, existing as one entity. For example, in a traditional farmhouse the internal floor was often continued outside under the eaves in order to ease the transition between interior and exterior. Houses are often separated from the garden only by *shoji*, which are screens 'glazed' with paper. During mild weather the screens are pulled right back, making the garden and room one visual space (as shown below). One reason for this is that in Japan both houses and gardens tend to be small in comparison to their Western

counterparts, due to the scarcity of land that can be built on. Fences or walls surround gardens, making them very private spaces, but as far as possible the house and garden are linked, continuing that harmonious relationship that the Japanese have with nature.

Application to Western Spaces

Throughout their history the Japanese have created gardens in all types of spaces, from acres of ground during the Heian period to the narrow path areas that dominate tea gardens. However, as many of the historical gardens from the Muromachi period onwards tended to be small in scale, and gardens associated with private houses were limited in size, the brilliance of Japanese gardens has been quite rightly attributed to small spaces. When asked to think of a typical Japanese garden, most people will imagine a courtyard, probably gravelled, containing bamboo and perhaps a stone lantern.

Such a design is ideal for a courtyard or restricted space where light is often limited, and its simplicity and restraint are inherently Japanese and admirably appropriate. One wall on to the courtyard may be glazed, and what could be better than having a view which, like a scroll painting, unfolds as your eyes move from left to right.

Larger spaces can also be used to good effect. They can be divided into small-scale units, perhaps each with a different theme. Alternatively, they can be treated as one large space through which the participant strolls in order to experience it all. A degree of enclosure and variety can be achieved by modelling or contouring the ground.

Certain Western building styles lend themselves more readily than others to Japanese ideas in the surrounding garden – for example, those with clean, crisp lines that are simple in design, perhaps with parts glazed down to the floor. Overhanging eaves help to connect the building to the garden, as does a verandah or timber platform raised above garden level. It is difficult to give precise guidance but, as ever, it requires a sensitive approach to achieve harmony.

If you are proposing to design a garden for someone else, remember that the experience it creates for the user is all-important. The sense of visual harmony, sensory experience, inspiration or spiritual awakening it may evoke is dependent on the user. Their psyche, their desires and aspirations should be assessed so that they will feel right in the garden. A garden designed for another person might be quite different.

From inside a building, the shoji *or paper screens create enclosure and control the extent of the sky and garden composition that can be seen.*

chapter 2

Traditional Garden Styles

Historical gardens can provide us with a wealth of inspiration, just as they have done garden designers through the centuries. As an art, and as an important part of the culture of a particular period in history, Japan's historical gardens provide a valuable insight into the influences prevailing at that time. A study of them reveals both a deeper understanding of the underlying principles and aesthetic and practical ideas for creating new gardens and landscapes.

The periods in Japanese history that are important to gardens are as follows:

784–1185	Heian period
1185–1392	Kamakura period
1392–1568	Muromachi period
1568–1615	Momoyama period
1615–1867	Edo period

Kinkaku-ji or the Golden Pavilion is a paradise garden dominated by the three-storey pavilion mirrored in the lakes. The pine-clad island in the middle distance is an important element in the overall design.

Shinto Influences

The word for garden, *niwa*, first appeared in the *Nihon-Shoki,* or Chronicles of Japan, compiled in the early eighth century, where its use indicated a place for the worship of gods. At that time, the indigenous rituals and beliefs, loosely termed Shinto, called for the worship of natural objects and ancestors. Spirits were brought down to the earth by rituals that took place in sacred compounds with a ground covering of pebbles, enclosed by ropes. The compound was normally bare except for a sacred tree.

The Ise shrine, in the mountains of central Japan, is an example of a sanctified precinct where the vacant site, a gravel area with only a heart post (a timber post left from the previous building), to the left of the shrine, gives an impression of the early sacred compounds. Having been used continuously for worship since before the seventh century, it has a potent spiritual presence that cannot fail to touch the visitor. The shrine buildings are adjacent to the vacant site. Every twenty years new buildings are erected on the vacant site according to detailed instructions, the old buildings are demolished and the area cleared except for the heart post, and this then becomes the vacant site.

Natural objects such as mountains, streams, waterfalls, rocks and trees were thought to be inhabited by sacred *kami*, or spirits, which warranted worship. Any objects that had a particularly unusual shape were also revered and were wrapped in holy straw ropes to indicate their importance. Rocks are often treated like this (see p.30), and are sometimes protected by a small building. Mountains were considered particularly important, as they were inhabited both by *kami* and by people's ancestors.

Mount Fuji is the most famous mountain in Japan, with its distinctive conical shape. Over the centuries it has inspired many garden designers and painters. Artificial mountains in gardens were often built with shrines on them for the *kami* that originally dwelled in the garden. The presence of hills

A sketch from Josiah Conder's Landscape Gardening in Japan *(1893), showing lake and hill scenery from the Middle Kingdom in China — the inspiration for some aspects of Japanese garden design.*

Chinese Influences

in gardens was probably influenced by the very early Japanese custom of burying chiefs and princes in grave mounds surrounded by a small lake. The grave mounds were basically hills containing stone-lined tombs, and are thus similar to prehistoric earthworks found in Britain.

Other clues as to the origin of elements later used in gardens can also be found in the shrine compounds. As the gravel precincts or sanctified objects were centres for worship, the worshippers needed to purify themselves before entering. The purifying element was water, which may have been present in the form of a waterfall or stream, or otherwise was used out of a water bowl. The worshippers would wash their hands and rinse their mouths, as is still done to this day.

During the seventh century, there was a great deal of movement by members of the nobility and priesthood between Japan, Korea and China. This had an influence on Japan and garden design in a number of ways. Buddhism was introduced from China via Korea, but it was Indian Buddhism, which had in turn been modified by China's religious concepts and culture. As Buddhism came to be accepted in Japan, so temple craftsmen including garden constructors were brought over from China.

The first historical suggestion of what we could call a garden is recorded in the *Nihon-Shoki*, when a man called Roji-no-Takumi arrived from the Korean kingdom of Paekche in about the year 606. He apparently created artificial hills representing Mount Sumeru, the mythical mountain in the Buddhist universe, together with a connecting bridge in an area to the south of the imperial residence. Then, in 620, a garden is known to have been completed within the palace of Saga-no-Umako, with a man-made pond and island.

China had many other philosophies that were to influence Japanese gardens. In the landscape, the Chinese

Left: These 'wedded rocks' at Futami, joined by holy straw ropes, exemplify the Japanese belief that certain natural elements are inhabited by sacred spirits.

Below: The atmosphere at the Ise shrine, with its vacant site, is highly charged and is further proof that stones and trees can be a potent spiritual force.

Right: Mount Fuji, seen here from Gigoku Dam in Hakone, is such an intrinsic part of Japanese culture that it is frequently reproduced in gardens and paintings.

saw the workings of the great universal forces, such as Yin and Yang — Yin being the female, deep, destructive, negative side and Yang the male, high, constructive, positive side. It was believed that all universal things oscillate between these opposites, and landscape design sought to balance these opposites to create harmony.

Landscape painting in China typically showed elements of heaven, earth and also a human form or something man-made. By always including a human element in any picture the Chinese painters were proposing a scenario where man was in harmony with heaven and earth. The figure depicted both in painting and literature was frequently a hermit in a retreat, living in complete harmony with his environment. The hermit was shown, sometimes with an attendant, dwelling in a simple thatched hut amid wild nature. In the sixteenth century, the tea house came to be modelled on such a hermit's retreat.

Geomancy, or 'the art of adapting residences of the living and the dead so as to co-operate and harmonize with the local currents of cosmic breath' (Mitchell Bring, *Japanese Gardens, Design and Meaning*), was another universal force that was important to the Chinese. The cosmic breath, or *chi'i* energy, had to be mapped out for a particular site before anything could be built. This ran through the earth rather as veins and acupuncture points do through the human body. Orientation was the main factor affecting the energy of a site, and the Chinese used a type of compass for determining this.

The geomancer would make an evaluation of the site, noting down all the landscape features and their importance, and would then put forward proposals for the building positions and associated landscape. It was believed that the Yin and Yang could be balanced by building a pond or an artificial hill, or a pagoda might be erected as a kind of giant acupuncture needle to stimulate the *chi'i* energy.

Geomancers had a practical function in environmental terms. For instance, they would often recommend a south-facing site protected by a horseshoe-shaped mountain on the north, east and west sides. They advised positioning a dwelling in the 'belly of the dragon', that is on the inside of a bend in the river where the bank does not tend to erode. Tree planting was often suggested to achieve the favoured sheltered, and therefore calm, site. For gardens on a small scale, materials such as rocks, trees, water and soil had to be harmonized, as they affected the *chi'i* energy.

The *Sakuteiki*, or Book of Garden, was an eleventh-century gardening manual, believed to have been written by Tachibana-no-Toshitsuna; a supplement was added in 1289. In the book many geomantic principles were laid down which demonstrate the influence of the Chinese:

> *... the inner side of the curving stream represents the belly of the dragon and that the dwelling house built on that side foretells good luck, while placing the house on the outer side of the curve, or the back of the dragon, brings ill luck to the dweller. There is another doctrine of directing the water coming from the north straight to the south. This probably means that the north denotes the element of water, and the south fire. The harmony will be affected by the meeting of Yin(in) and Yang(yo) or the positive and negative. Thus the practice is not without reason.*
>
> *(translated by Shigemaru Shimoyama)*

The *Sakuteiki* also quotes a 'certain Chinese person of the Sung dynasty', suggesting that they were an authority, and again emphasizing the importance of China.

Many allegories and myths came to Japan from China, such as the tale of the mystic isles where immortals were thought to dwell. The concept of immortality had long been sought by the Chinese, as this delightful tale shows.

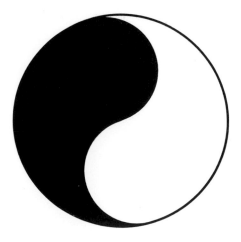

The 'two regulating powers which together create all the phenomena of Nature'.

The turtle island in the upper garden at Saiho-ji is aged by a covering of moss.

Apparently, there were five beautiful islands off the coast of Shantung, where all birds and beasts were the purest white, the trees bore pearls and other gems, every flower was fragrant and the fruits brought immortality to those who ate them. The inhabitants were humans who had attained immortality and who would fly around on the backs of cranes. As the islands were not fixed to the sea-bed they floated around, and so the Ruler of the Universe commanded fifteen enormous turtles to support them on their backs (note the importance of threes and fives). This was all right until one day a giant gathered up six of the turtles in a net, which allowed two of the islands to drift away, leaving three remaining islands.

Emperor Wu of Han tried to entice such immortals to his own estate with a lake and a number of rocky islands, including three mystic isles, and some rocks suggesting giant turtles. In the end, Emperor Wu proved to be mortal, but the allegory lives on in the frequent inclusion of mystic isles in paintings and in the gardens of Japan. Crane and turtle islands have been used in many gardens since, partly inspired by the tale and partly by the fact that they are thought to bring the concept of longevity into the gardens, as both are reputed to live very long lives. The typical layout of such islands is described in Chapter 4.

In Buddhism, Mount Sumeru is the mountain at the centre of the cosmos, around which there are apparently seven mountain ranges and seven seas. The Japanese called Mount Sumeru 'Shumisen', and in early gardens it was a feature that was frequently represented by a stone hill centrally located. By the fourteenth century, however, its significance had declined, as can be seen by the small size of the rock representing Shumisen at Kinkaku-ji.

As well as allegories and myths, travellers to China brought back lasting impressions of coastal scenery, and these had an important influence on gardens during the Heian period. Thus there were re-creations or suggestions of the pine-clad islets of Matsushima and the famous Ama-no-hashidate sand spit in the Tango province.

Although the Japanese imported ideas from China, they were rarely incorporated raw into Japanese gardens. Instead, the idea was taken and assimilated by the Japanese, influenced by Japan's own culture, native religion, climate and natural environment. The results were completely new elements that were totally Japanese and that were developed and refined over time in the design of gardens. For instance, the Japanese use rocks in their gardens, but never the craggy, eroded types with holes and hollows favoured by the Chinese. Instead the Japanese prefer quieter shapes with level tops. The high arched bridges characteristic of Chinese gardens were constructed during the Heian period but were later modified into lower, more modest shapes.

Paradise Gardens

Buddhist ideas began to have a direct influence on garden design during the Heian period when the Pure Land, or Jodo sect, of Buddhism was introduced from China. It taught that the chanting of the Buddha Amida's name would ensure re-birth in the paradise of the Pure Land. Such a paradise was not an intellectual concept but was believed to be a physical reality, with beautiful pavilions standing among ponds of lotus blossoms, where the immortals passed their time in boats drifting among the flowers and celestial music. It was an image of peace and harmony readily taken up both in court circles and among the populace in a period that was dotted with civil disorder.

Paradise was represented in paintings to give Buddhist followers a taste of the bliss awaiting them in the next world. These images were soon translated into physical realities, which in themselves were important developments in temple and garden design. Initially the arrangements were simple lotus ponds in front of a central building, but with time the layouts became more complex and elaborate.

Byodo-in

The Phoenix Hall at Byodo-in, Uji, situated on the west bank of a lotus pond, is the best remaining example of a central hall housing an Amida Buddha. The hall is thought to resemble a phoenix about to take flight. The original garden no longer exists, but it was thought to have a Seven Treasure pond filled with lotuses, with bridges linking the various parts of the garden, as depicted in Jodo paradise paintings.

Byodo-in was an example of a Shinden-style mansion. This was, typically, a complex of structures connected by roofed corridors, raised above ground level. The main hall of the mansion was located on the north side with the garden to the south (see opposite). The main hall, or Shinden, was flanked by buildings for family quarters, and the garden was enclosed by roofed corridors running into small pavilions raised up over the pond. These pavilions had names such as Fishing Hall or Spring Hall. The forecourt in front of the Shinden was kept clear for entertainments and

for people paying their respects to the lord of the mansion.

An idea of this design can be gained from the Shishin-den at Kyoto Imperial Palace (as shown opposite), which is a nineteeth-century reconstruction of the original, researched from old records. The courtyard facing the Shinden is stunningly simple, being surfaced with white gravel and containing only two trees — one a mandarin orange and the other a cherry. The roofed corridors around the courtyard show a Chinese influence, but the shingle roof and white gravel are typically Japanese. Other important characteristics of the Shinden-style landscape were a stream that ran under one of the corridors and out into the garden, with associated bridge and rocks; a pond with islands reached by bridges; and sometimes a central hill representing Shumisen. The direction in which the stream flowed was influenced by Chinese thinking and, as laid down in the *Sakuteiki*, it should flow from left to right as one sat in the Shinden.

Within the complex, small open courts called *tsubo* were left in front of the more important rooms. Planting tended to be showy, with tubs of flowering plants in the Chinese style, and ladies whose rooms were adjacent to the *tsubo* became known by the name of the dominant flower. Thus there is Lady Fujitsubo, or She of the Wisteria Chamber, in the Tale of Genji.

Tachibana-no-Toshitsuna, the author of the *Sakuteiki*, was the son of Fujiwara, who built Byodo-in. The book describes the principles of Shinden-style gardens and reveals how, by the twelfth century, the Japanese had developed ideas taken from Chinese gardens into their own distinctive style.

Opposite: The Shishin-den at Kyoto Imperial Palace evokes aspects of the Shinden style and shows a well-orchestrated simplicity in the design of its surrounding spaces.

The Phoenix Hall at Byodo-in, Uji, a Shinden-style mansion which gives an impression of a paradise garden (although the original garden no longer exists).

Saiho-ji

Saiho-ji, also called Kokedera or the Moss Temple, is one of the oldest surviving gardens in Japan, with great presence. It was originally laid out as a paradise garden of the Jodo sect in the twelfth century with, it is thought, two temples illustrating the dual concepts of the sect — the sinful world and the Pure Land. Edo-ji, or the Temple of (Aloofness from) the Foul World, was placed on the hillside and Saiho-ji, or the Temple of the Westward Direction (Amida's paradise), was placed on level ground where it was possible to construct a pond.

The Buddhist priest Muso Soseki (1275–1351) was commissioned in later years to convert Saiho-ji into a Zen temple. He changed one of the Chinese characters in the name, so that instead of meaning Temple of the Westward Direction (alluding to the Pure Land of the western paradise), it came to mean Temple of the Western Fragrance. He re-designed the garden and built halls and pavilions. Flowering trees that were present when it was a paradise garden were allowed to die and were not replaced, to emphasize Zen aesthetics, of which we will learn more later. The main structure standing on the west side of the golden pond was the Sheri-den, an impressive two-storey building, the lower storey being known as the Ruri-den.

None of these buildings exists now, but an idea of their concept can be gained from the pavilion at Kinkaku-ji, which was modelled on the Sheri-den, and at Ginkaku-ji, which was modelled on the Ruri-den. The pond was designed to focus attention on the Sheri-den and to suggest a Buddhist paradise. A line of night-mooring stones suggests a chain of boats anchored for the night.

A gateway divides the lower garden from the upper garden, and indeed the older paradise garden from the Zen-inspired garden above. Here, climbing up the hillside, one comes upon a *karesansui*, or dry landscape, which at the time of construction was truly innovative and was the beginning of a technique that has been used right up to the present day. Rocks were set to suggest the falling and splashing of water down a cascade, although water never actually ran. This full-scale feature is very powerful indeed, perhaps more so because of the lack of water. The composition continues 'downstream' with two pools, and a flat stone alongside used for meditation. Further down there is another rock composition in the form of a turtle, a reminder of the mystic isles that were supported on the backs of turtles in Chinese mythology.

The garden also introduced another innovation. Paths were built to allow people to stroll around the garden rather than be confined, as previously, to views from the interior of a building or from boats. Today the garden has an atmosphere of great serenity, which comes partly from its religious use over the centuries and partly from its gentle moss covering and the sea of tree trunks that draw the eye to infinity. Trees have generally not been trained, but allowed to grow naturally, and the constant filtering of light by the overhead evergreen trees adds to the atmosphere.

The sculptural log bridge at Saiho-ji leads the viewer's eye across the pond. The rich moss growth and overhead shade combine to form a garden of great serenity and age.

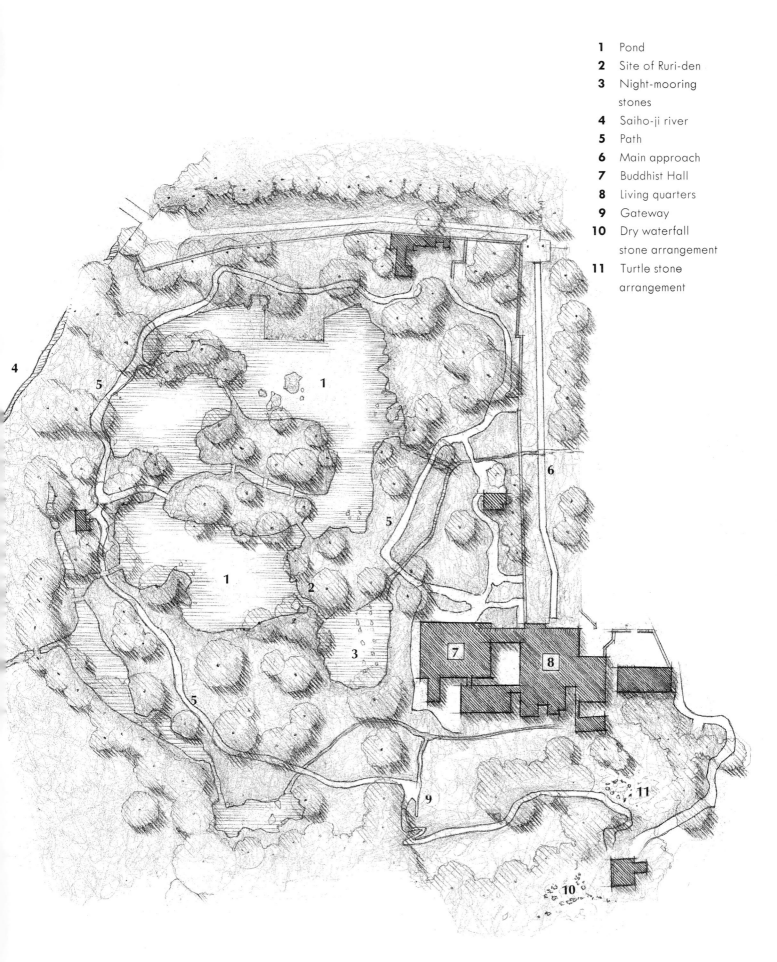

1 Pond
2 Site of Ruri-den
3 Night-mooring
   stones
4 Saiho-ji river
5 Path
6 Main approach
7 Buddhist Hall
8 Living quarters
9 Gateway
10 Dry waterfall
   stone arrangement
11 Turtle stone
   arrangement

Kinkaku-ji

Kinkaku-ji, or the Golden Pavilion, displays a strange fusion of the elements of a paradise garden, with a pond, and Chinese grandeur, as epitomized by the pavilion itself. It was built by Yoshimitsu in 1397, modelled on the Sheri-den at Saiho-ji. He situated the pavilion in a pond, connected to the other buildings by corridors. The pond has stone arrangements representing the nine mountains and eight seas of the Buddhist myth, and was originally used for boating purposes. The three-storey pavilion, which is mirrored in the pond, now stands on the shore due to silting up in later years. The other buildings in the complex were either moved or burnt down, but Kinkaku-ji survived until 1950 when it was destroyed by fire. An accurate replica was constructed in 1955 and still stands today.

From the pavilion, the lake appears to be larger than it really is. This is achieved by some clever techniques, which are discussed in detail in Chapter 3. The lake is divided into two parts, with the inner part filled with rocks and islands to give interest to the eye, and the outer part kept empty and only vaguely perceived in the distance. The division is created by a peninsula, jutting out from the shore (as shown in the plan on p.41), together with a long island and a group of pine trees — trimmed to keep them in scale. The shoreline is formed by groups of fine stones. Beyond the island in the outer part of the lake are a number of scattered islands purposefully designed to be small to create an illusion of distance from the pavilion.

Most of the islands are turtle islands — low in profile, with rocks as legs jutting out. One turtle island is partnered with a crane island. This crane island was constructed merely as a group of medium-height rocks with flat tops, whereas later examples of crane islands were basically just a vertical rock. Like the rock composition in the *karesansui* at Saiho-ji, these islands are a reference to the mystic isles myth. Also similar to Saiho-ji is the line of night-mooring stones which lie by the pavilion. On the hillside is a Dragon Gate Cascade (dry) with the famous carp stone at its base, constructed in the thirteenth century. The stone is beginning its ascent to dragonhood, so the tale goes.

Right: The three-storey Golden Pavilion at Kinkaku-ji at sunset. Erected by the Ashikaga shogun Yoshimitsu, a leader in garden building, it was converted into a Zen temple after his death.

Left: Waterfalls are a common natural feature of Japan's mountains and consequently an important element in garden composition. The fall of this dramatic cascade at Kinkaku-ji is effectively broken by a stone at the base, heightening the impact.

1 Golden Pavilion
2 Temple buildings
3 Mirror pond
4 Path
5 Night-mooring stones
6 Route to upper pond

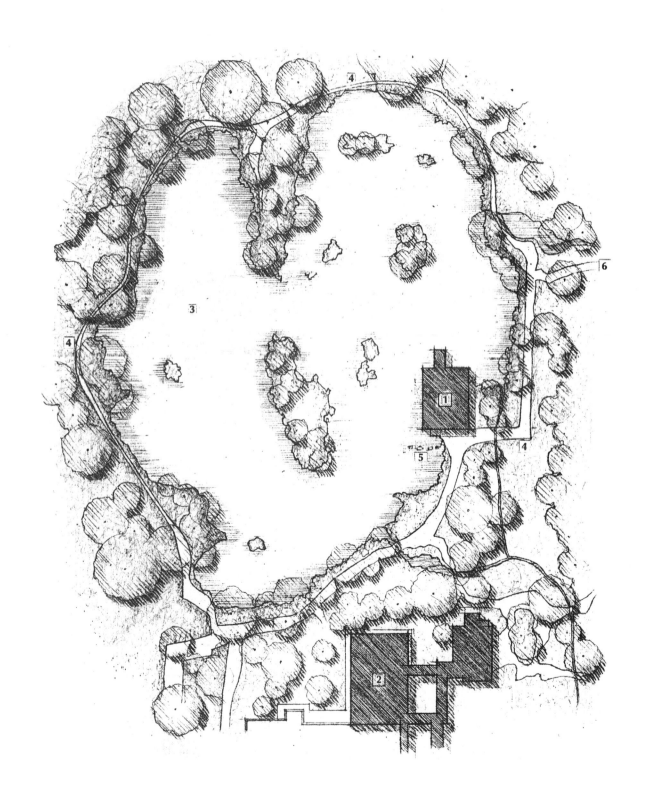

Above: The lower garden at Ginkaku-ji, showing the scale of the pond and the restrained style of the pavilion.

Right: The flat-topped gravel cone on a bed of raked sand at Ginkaku-ji is in keeping with the Zen aesthetic.

Ginkaku-ji

Ginkaku-ji, or the Silver Pavilion (or alternatively Jisho-ji), was much smaller in scale and more restrained than Saiho-ji or Kinkaku-ji, showing the increasing influence of Zen Buddhism on the arts. It is thought to have been designed by Yoshimasa (1435–90), grandson of the builder of Kinkaku-ji, and completed in 1493. At the time, there was a great deal of interest in Saiho-ji and an official record shows that Yoshimasa visited it often and on one occasion exclaimed, 'The beauty of this garden never diminishes' (Loraine Kuck, *The World of the Japanese Garden*). Twelve structures were completed, including a monumental gate, curved bridge, covered corridors, a chapel, study, reception hall and several pavilions. All that remains now is the main hall of Ginkaku-ji and a small Amida chapel called Togu-do.

Ginkaku-ji was a direct copy of the Ruri-den at Saiho-ji, with a Buddhist deity housed in the upper storey. Looking from the balcony of the pavilion, the eye is led along the outline of the trees in the background to a definite dip, where the moon is reputed to rise. As at Saiho-ji, the garden is divided into two parts, the pond and buildings in the lower garden and the stone composition above. There is an overall feeling of Zen restraint and the desire for that which is simple and natural, and this developed increasingly with later gardens. The pond is small with a complex shape and several islands, and was therefore not intended for

boating parties; instead, paths were provided for strolling along. The hillside spring at Ginkaku-ji was a direct copy of the one at Saiho-ji, with similar-shaped rocks around it. The cascade called the Moon Washing Spring, standing on the hillside, hints of the one at Kinkaku-ji.

As with many gardens, the stones and plants for Ginkaku-ji were taken from existing gardens. In fact, in later years some were removed from Ginkaku-ji to make others. Records show that a well-known garden constructor called Zen'ami was involved in building the garden. His name also appears as the builder of other gardens in the fifteenth century; in fact, he was probably the first of a class of professional garden-makers.

Today, the most startling part of the garden is a huge flat-topped cone of white gravel and a white patterned gravel bed. Much discussion has revolved around these artefacts, as it is not known when they first appeared. However, successive woodcuts in books from the seventeenth century to the nineteenth century show the gravel piles getting larger. The idea behind them is also not clear, but it has been speculated that the sand bed's purpose was to reflect moonlight into the pavilion.

Ginkaku-ji marks a turning point in Japanese garden design, containing aspects of a refined early garden style, yet introducing new elements that were to feature increasingly in later gardens.

A view from the Abbot's Quarters at Tenryu-ji, with the land jutting out into the pond on the right, a dry waterfall with bridge, and a Sung-style island group of seven angular rocks at the rear. Originally the background was a shakkei to the hills of Arashiyama beyond.

Tenryu-ji

Like Ginkaku-ji, Tenryu-ji is a Shinden-style pond garden but on a much smaller scale, and introducing new elements that later became popular. It also has one of the best examples of Chinese-influenced rock groups. The garden is thought to have been laid out by Soseki, who was also responsible for Saiho-ji. It can be divided into three parts: the foreground, middle distance and background. This structure is similar to the planes in Chinese paintings, as explained later in Chapter 3. In the foreground is an area of level gravel, relating to the similar but larger area of gravel in front of the Shinden-style mansions. In the middle distance is a pond with land jutting out from the side, which helps to increase the spaciousness. Towards the rear of the pond are the focal points of dry waterfall, bridge and island rock group. The background is an enclosing hill and trees that merge into the hills beyond, but at one time comprised *shakkei*, or borrowed scenery (see Chapter 3).

The dry waterfall is best viewed from the bridge in front of it. Its water-falling stone has an ideal notch in the top and striations down the face that immediately suggest falling water. (The water-falling stone is the most important stone in the waterfall and it is from this that the water is first seen to fall, or appears to fall in a dry waterfall.) The bridge, composed of natural stone slabs, crosses in front of the fall and visually balances the composition. Rocks placed around the fall give a sense of depth and mystery to the gorge; above the fall is a sloping area of rapids, all dry; and then above this is a second fall, reinforcing the suggestion of a rushing water course. It has been postulated that water used to run in the fall, fed from the other side of the valley by an overhead conduit.

In front of the bridge is a striking rock island composed of seven angular rocks, obviously Sung in style and thought to have been constructed by some Chinese rock craftsmen who fled to Japan. The central peak is a pointed pinnacle, with flat-topped rocks around giving visual support and making the composition balanced from wherever it is viewed around the lake. The composition may be meant to represent the mystic isles, or indeed Mount Sumeru.

The background has not always enclosed the garden. Originally it was designed as *shakkei*, borrowing the hills of Arashiyama beyond. These were planted with cherry trees as a special feature of the garden. Henceforth, Arashiyama became a place to visit particularly at cherry blossom time, a reputation it has kept to the present day. However, the trees to the rear of the garden gradually grew so large that they obscured the *shakkei*, until in 1934 a storm brought down a lot of the large trees, revealing the view again.

The fact that the designer Soseki was responsible for both Saiho-ji and Tenryu-ji can be seen in the severity of the rock composition in both dry waterfalls. The reduced Heian-period pond, and new elements such as paths and bridges for strolling, put Tenryu-ji at a transitional point in garden tradition. Later gardens were to become even more reduced in scale, with *shakkei* being used more often.

The stone bridge at Tenryu-ji with the Sung-style rock composition creating an island in front. Balance is achieved when viewed from any position.

Zen Gardens

As the Pure Land, or Jodo sect of Buddhism began to lose its influence, the Zen Buddhist sect took root. Priests such as Eisai and Dogen travelled to China and on their return set up monasteries. This was a time when the influence of the nobility was reduced and power had passed to the warrior class. Zen became the main religion of this class during the Kamakura period.

Zen Buddhism is not easy to explain as it cannot be intellectualized – the practice of Zen takes one beyond the intellect. Rather than the reading of scriptures or devotional duties to achieve a state of enlightenment, or *satori*, the emphasis is on direct experience. Dogen said:

To learn the way of the Buddha is to learn about oneself.
To learn about oneself is to forget oneself.
To forget oneself is to be enlightened by everything in the world.
To be enlightened by everything is to let fall one's own body and mind.

Enlightenment is achieved by doing meditation, or *zazen*, for long periods under the direction of a master, thereby developing the mind to a level where it 'knows' by direct experience of the infinite. In this state one has an immediate insight into the nature of things rather than understanding through an intellectual process. As part of their practice Zen students confront such questions as, 'What is the sound of one hand clapping?' The normal mode of thinking is upset by such a question, as it cannot be comprehended by logic. Instead the student meditates on it.

Zen came to affect gardens in two ways: indirectly through Zen-inspired paintings and directly by Zen priest-gardeners designing gardens.

As Zen monks travelled back and forth from China during the fourteenth and fifteenth centuries, they brought back Chinese Sung paintings, which influenced Japanese Muromachi-period painters. Their style was mainly monochrome using black ink on semi-absorbent paper, where each brush stroke was distinct and final. The paintings of the Zen monk Sesshu (as seen opposite) clearly show this. They chose to draw dramatic mountains with cliffs and peaks, with pines clinging to the rocks, rivers and villages down below, and steep winding paths climbing up the hillsides. These paintings were filled with Zen symbolism: the hemmed-in human existence in the dark valleys, with the paths rising up to inspiring peaks of enlightenment.

The scenes were not representational; instead, the artist studied the landscape and attempted to extract the essential nature of the elements and then present them on paper. The painting technique often used straight or angular strokes to convey the feeling of rock, as can be seen in Sesshu's paintings. Muromachi garden designers were inspired by such paintings and many flat-topped rocks feature in their compositions. As in paintings, rock arrangements were sometimes used simply to create rhythm in the garden rather than to symbolize a waterfall or shoreline. The miniature landscapes created in compositions were often taken from paintings and were therefore basically Chinese in origin.

The other effect of Zen was the direct one of priest-gardeners, such as Sesshu and Soami, designing gardens to illustrate a particular Zen concept, or for the purpose of *zazen* (meditation). Incidentally, these priests were both painters and gardeners. In just the same way that the essential nature of the elements was extracted in painting, the essence of the garden elements had to be brought out.

To do this, the style of 'heaven on earth' Heian paradise gardens, with their elaborate ponds, waterfalls, trees and shrubs, was laid aside. Instead, the Zen aesthetic of simplifying everything to its essential nature by suggestion and symbolism was adopted, allowing the mind space for imagination and contemplation. In practical terms this was achieved by various forms of abstraction involving a reduction in scale and a restraint in the use of materials, and is best explained by reference to some of the gardens.

Reaction to such gardens is bound to differ among people with different previous experiences, background (what Jung would call their unconscious mind) and frame of mind when entering the space. However, even someone uninitiated in Zen or other spiritual practices should sense in them something very powerful and moving.

The beginnings of the Zen influence can be seen at Saiho-ji, Ginkaku-ji and Tenryu-ji, but the art was perfected in the gardens of Daisen-in and Ryoan-ji.

Autumn *from* A Picture of Mountain and Water in Four Seasons *by Sesshu Toyo. This graphically illustrates the artist's profound concern with Zen symbolism, showing humans struggling along steep paths and rugged mountains to achieve the peaks of enlightenment. Also shown is the artist's seal.*

47

Daisen-in

As a sub-temple of Daitoku-ji in Kyoto, Daisen-in contains a brilliant *karesansui*, or dry landscape garden, composed merely of rocks, gravel and a few carefully chosen plants. It takes its inspiration from paintings and is pervaded by the spirit of Zen.

The composition is centred around the image of a water course that begins in the mountains as a waterfall, drops into a stream, and flows into a river, eventually becoming the sea. As one looks out from the Abbot's Quarters, the eye is drawn to the focus of the composition in the left-hand corner. This is a group of rugged rocks, set to the north-east, which suggest tall mountains and are reminiscent of those portrayed in Sung paintings. A dry waterfall, represented by a striated rock, gushes out of the mountain, (see opposite) falls on to some pools of gravel, and then one arm of it flows under a low stone-slab bridge. The bridge, like the one at Tenryu-ji, has a balancing influence on the rock groups behind and suggests a path leading up to the mountains.

The stream, symbolized by gravel and raked to suggest motion, flows down to the right and turns into an upland river, with the verandah as the near shore and rocks as the far shore, passing crane and turtle islands on its way. It then flows under a corridor bridge that was re-constructed in 1961 after research into old records. Further downstream it becomes a more placid river, with a rock in the shape of a junk seemingly bobbing up and down in the 'water'. Finally, the river reaches the far right of the 'picture', where it flows under the verandah to the southern garden. The large rectangular bed of raked gravel here is said to represent the Great Sea (see pp.52–3). It is punctuated only by two white gravel cones, which are thought to have been formed by surplus material left there temporarily after raking, but which over the years have become permanent.

The second arm of the stream runs around to the north of the building, passing large rocks that suggest giant cliffs, and ends in a drainage area of cobbles with an early form of stone arrangement for washing.

The garden is a very tight space, enclosed on one side by the temple with its large overhanging eaves and a verandah below, and on the other by a simple white wall with pantile coping. The temple is in the Shoin style, so when the screens, or *shoji*, of the building are drawn back, the room opens directly on to the verandah and garden space. Behind the mountain composition, which suggests Mount Shumisen, are clipped evergreen shrubs acting as a backcloth, with trees behind.

The garden was constructed soon after the building, which was completed in 1513. The designers are thought to have been Soami and the founder of the temple, Kogaken. The use of gravel to symbolize water is part of the Zen aesthetic of distilling elements to their essence, encouraging the viewer to set aside the limits of physical appearance and reality, and drawing the mind to a conceptual state where contemplation and meditation flow.

An impressive depth and spaciousness were achieved in this garden of only 70 square metres (753 sq ft). The techniques of miniaturization, rock arrangement, composition and balance are all beautifully orchestrated and provided inspiration for later gardens. Seated on the verandah with a quiet mind, you find the full power of the composition revealed to you.

left: A close-up of the striking dry waterfall rock group at Daisen-in. Water from the mountain appears to tumble over various falls in a very accomplished fashion. Such a composition could only have been designed by a Zen master.

Below: The water course at Daisen-in prior to its reconstruction by Kinsaku Nakane in 1961. Following old records, Professor Nakane re-created the roofed bridge, as shown overleaf (right).

The visual simplicity and balance of this rock composition at Daisen-in are masterful. The contrasts, from gravel to rock to hemp screen, continue the Zen aesthetic.

The water course at Daisen-in, as seen from a seated position in the Abbot's Quarters. Water appears to flow from the dry waterfall in the left-hand corner, under the roofed bridge, and out through the river on the right.

Overleaf: A Zen monk contemplates the white expanse of raked gravel in the Great Sea Garden of Daisen-in, a vast space punctuated only by two cones of excess material. The formless gravel frees the mind and allows it to expand.

51

Ryoan-ji

The rock garden of Ryoan-ji is one further stage of abstraction and, as such, is a masterpiece. The composition is laid out on a flat rectangular area in front of the *hojo*, or main hall, enclosed on the other sides by an earthen wall with a tile roof. It is viewed only from the verandah or from the room that borders it. Fifteen rocks in five groups rise up out of the gravel bed. Each individual group is a perfectly balanced composition, as is one group in relation to another group, and altogether they appear to flow from left to right. This is achieved by the rocks standing at a slight slant, except for one group that appears to be flowing against the current. It would be impossible to remove a single stone without ruining the whole effect.

The gravel is raked in straight parallel lines except for the areas around the rocks, where lines follow the contours in just the same way that, in a current, water eddies around a rock (see opposite). No trees or shrubs are in evidence, but there are patches of moss at the base of the rocks that soften the austerity of the composition and provide a seat for the rocks. The garden looks particularly vibrant after rain when the moisture brings out the colours of the different elements.

Speculation as to the meaning of the garden abounds, ranging from tiger cubs crossing a river, islands in a sea (with possibly the Inland Sea as the inspiration), to mountain tops above the clouds. Its designer is not known for certain, but Soami (one of the designers of Daisen-in) has been suggested, and two garden workers whose names are inscribed on one of the stones probably did the actual construction.

The masterful composition of fifteen rocks on a gravel bed at Ryoan-ji demonstrates the simplicity and abstraction of Zen Buddhism at its highest level. Each rock group is perfectly balanced, and together they seem to flow from left to right. The enclosing wall removes distractions from beyond.

Some authorities consider that the garden once included a view of a distant hill, using the framing of tree trunks in the *shakkei* manner. Another has found evidence that the garden once had cherry trees planted in it, which were its main focus. Further discussion revolves around the colour of the walls, which are now dull earth colours but are thought to have been white originally.

Whatever the theories and controversies, Ryoan-ji remains a garden of extreme abstraction where complete harmony prevails, and absolute simplification and refinement have been reached. The garden can only express that stage of Zen known as *satori*, or enlightenment. There are no elements for the mind to hang on to, so thoughts are just suspended in space. Most visitors are simply left in awe.

The raking of gravel around rocks in Japanese gardens resembles water eddying around a rock in a lake and gives inspiration and meaning to the composition. In Zen philosophy, still water (the mind) reflects reality purely, but as soon as a stone (thought) makes ripples, reality becomes distorted.

Tea Gardens

The unique tradition of tea gardens had a great influence on later gardens through their atmosphere, the elements used and their relevance to small-scale spaces. Like Zen gardens, the inspiration for tea gardens came from China but quickly developed into something very Japanese and was completely integrated into their culture.

Tea was a common beverage in China in the T'ang period (618–907), but the practice of drinking powdered tea was brought to Japan by Zen monks in order to reduce sleepiness during meditation. The tea leaves were ground down, hot water added, and then the mixture was whipped into a froth. The result is quite bitter and definitely an acquired taste! The monks drank the powdered tea from a common bowl in ceremonial fashion. The military aristocracy then took up the practice and held gatherings where guests would sip various kinds of tea and try to identify them. Yoshimasa held such gatherings of artists at Ginkaku-ji and he was advised on aesthetic matters by Shuko, a Zen monk (1423–1502). The artistic ideals of the Muromachi period were ones of restraint and simplicity, and Shuko developed basic ways of serving tea directed by the host, and advised on the atmosphere to be created.

Part of the Togu-do pavilion at Ginkaku-ji was adapted for the purpose of tea drinking and many of the features of room design, utensils and ornaments were forerunners of later styles. At this time, the garden was not specifically designed for tea gatherings.

The great tea master Sen no Rikyu (1520–91) later laid down further principles important in the 'way of tea'. He was a Zen practitioner, flower arranger and a recognized connoisseur of good taste, whose opinions were sought by the great leaders such as Hideyoshi. Under Rikyu, the distinct style of tea gardens was developed, inspired partly by the typical Chinese hermit's retreat, or by huts in the mountains. A poem by Fujiwara-no-Sadare sums up the scene:

> *In the distance*
> *Neither flowers or maple leaves*
> *Are to be seen*
> *Only a thatched hut beside the bay*
> *In autumn's twilight.*

Below: The characteristic roof structure of Japanese farmhouses influenced the tea house's rustic appearance.

Right: Sen no Rikyu (1520–91), the great tea master whose philosophy inspired many famous tea gardens.

三玄春屋文宗園

文禄第四乙未歳舍季穐念四日

上完香供云

宗慶熙之請賀伽陀一絶係

利休居士肖像常題信男

斯翁事必知

旧時姿趙州且坐喫茶底有不

頭上申兼手中扇傳然遺像

Rikyu emphasized the importance of materials that were simple and rustic, but also refined, so that everything was perfectly clean. The path to the tea house was the *roji*, or dewy path, and had to seem like an untrodden way through wild landscape to a hermit's hut. The tea house itself had a predominantly natural appearance, inspired partly by Japanese farmhouses, and was made from natural materials such as thatch and timber left in the round.

Two particular qualities had to pervade the tea garden — *wabi* and *sabi*. *Wabi* is solitude among nature, and *sabi* an atmosphere of age. The journey along the path was intended as a psychological cleansing, leaving worldly cares behind, so that one entered into a quieter and more serene state of mind, as was necessary for the tea ceremony. The sequence of small areas in a typical tea garden, divided by gates and fences, is part of the process of preparing the guests' minds: the outer garden, with the waiting chamber or bench, is nearer to the outside world, whereas the inner gardens have cast off civilization and are closer to nature.

The sequence of events in a typical tea ceremony is for the group of guests, usually numbering fewer than five, to assemble on the waiting bench in the outer garden. When the signal is given, they pass along the path to the tea house, stopping on the way to wash their hands and perhaps their mouths at a stone water basin (or *tsukubai*) in an act of purification of both body and mind. Outside the tea house there are flat stones on which the guests place their wooden clogs or shoes before bending down to enter in silence through the door of the tea house.

Once inside, there are no views of the garden and the guests go to the *tokonoma* to look at the painting or flower arrangement (see p.16), which may relate to the reason for the gathering. They then sit on the *tatami* (rush) mats to await their host, who enters and begins to make the powdered tea with slow, graceful movements, using special implements chosen for both practical and aesthetic reasons. The tea is served in a bowl of rough pottery, in keepng with the rustic atmosphere. Each guest sips the tea, quietly admires the bowl, and then returns it to the host. When all

Below, left: *The tea garden at Omote-Senke, divided by a series of gateways symbolizing the release of wordly cares and entry into the world of tea.*

Below, right: *The dewy path to the Fushin-an tea house at Omote Senke. Guests have to humble themselves by stooping through the low door of the tea house.*

Right: The tea house in Rikugien Garden, Tokyo (designed in 1695), gives the impression of a hermit's hut in a wild landscape.

the guests have drunk, conversation follows, but only that of a refined nature, avoiding subjects such as politics or business, which are considered inappropriate.

There are a number of important criteria to be borne in mind when creating a *roji*. Stepping stones are used to direct the way the guests walk, to focus their attention and to keep their feet clean. As the story goes, the use of stepping stones in tea gardens was invented by Dotei. Yoshimasa apparently stopped at Dotei's hermitage for a visit and had his attendants spread out a number of objects for him to walk on, presumably because the path was muddy. When he saw this, Dotei had the idea of using stepping stones at intervals for a garden path. The layout of stepping stones varies with the tea master, but generally they meander in a number of specific ways. This is discussed later in Chapter 4.

Other important features of tea gardens are the foot-stones that are placed under the 'waiting pavilion' for the guests' shoes. The main guest is given a larger, more elevated rock than the other guests. Gateways and fences should be made of natural materials such as bamboo or dried roots, to continue the atmosphere of *wabi* and *sabi*. The *tsukubai*, or water basin, was another essential element. It was not as tall as the *chozubachi*, which it replaced, and thus required the guests to humble themselves to use it. A particular stone arrangement should surround the water

The stone basin fed by running water and the bamboo ladle (like those shown at the Ise shrine) are essential elements of the cleansing ritual before entering the tea house.

basin, and this is explained in Chapter 4. As an alternative to a *tsukubai*, a spring directed through a bamboo pipe could be used. Ornamental stones were placed casually around the garden, as if they cropped out naturally but, of course, were actually positioned with the utmost care and sensitivity. Tea gardens did not, however, have the major stone groups or the waterfalls that were so important in other styles of gardens.

A *chiriana*, or waste hole, of small rocks set into the ground was usually provided for depositing leaves and twigs that had been collected during the raking and sweeping of the ground, which is always carried out before a tea ceremony. Although it is a principle that garden debris should be swept up, nevertheless a garden must always retain its naturalism. A delightful story comes to mind here which illustrates this.

Rikyu was teaching his son how to clean the garden and the boy had swept the garden debris from the paths and moss. However, each time he went to tell his father it was finished, Rikyu scolded him and said that it was not right. So his son swept again and again until not one leaf could be found on the ground, but Rikyu was still not satisfied. Then Rikyu went up to a maple tree full of leaves in autumn colour and shook the tree firmly. A few brilliant red leaves fluttered down on to the lush green moss carpet adding the subtle hint of naturalism. Rikyu then told his son that the scene was perfect.

Lighting was provided by stone lanterns that were specially developed for tea gardens, although some had been used already in temple grounds. The various types are explained in Chapter 4. Lanterns had to be both functional and aesthetic, and considerable care was taken with their design. They were located near waiting pavilions, water basins or tea houses, and a tallow candle provided the soft, gentle light needed to retain the atmosphere.

As for plants, only trees that would grow on wild hillsides were chosen, with a preference for broad-leaved evergreens because of their timeless quality. No bright or showy flowers, or plants with strong scents, were allowed except for the apricot, which blooms only modestly in early spring. The floor covering was moss, and ferns were planted around the base of rocks, just as they would grow in the wild.

All the elements were chosen with the utmost sensitivity and care so that they were in harmony with the atmosphere being cultivated. This sensitivity — together with a number of elements first developed in tea gardens, such as stepping stones, water basins and lanterns — was to be used in later gardens right through to the present day.

Katsura Detached Palace

In the garden of Katsura Detached Palace many elements and principles of the tea garden have been successfully integrated into a vast miniature landscape that directs the awareness of the mind as one wanders through it.

The lake is central to the garden and, being a complex shape with viewpoints winding off to unseen points, its actual size of 2 hectares (5 acres) can never be fully appreciated. Around the edge of the lake, the ground is contoured to create hills, which sweep down to the mostly soft edges of the lake shore. Residential buildings on the lake edge consist of the Old Shoin, Middle Shoin and New Palace, connected together.

One of the most important elements of the design are paths. These connect the pavilions and tea houses and direct pedestrians' feet as well as their minds. Stepping stones can be either natural or cut (dressed) stone, and are sometimes even long stone slabs. Their purpose is to cause people to walk in a particular manner. The straight lines of a cut-stone pavement leading to a water basin or waiting pavilion give way to stepping stones by a shore, which then wind up a hill and out of sight. At every turn and over every hill a new view is unfolded, rather like being shown a collection of landscape paintings. This, and the numerous bridges that one crosses over, gives the impression that the garden is limitless, and this feeling is reinforced by the fact that at no viewpoint can the whole garden be observed.

There are two tea houses within the garden at Katsura: the Shokintei and the Shokatei. The Shokintei looks out over a miniature representation of Ama-no-hashidate, the famous sand spit in China, which is a fine example of elements scaled down in size (see p.62). The small stone lantern, like a lighthouse on a promontory, is particularly appealing. There is a washing place adjacent to the lake for ritual hand-rinsing.

The other tea house, the Shokatei, is interesting in that its interior penetrates the exterior space. Tea houses often borrowed rustic elements from traditional Japanese farmhouses, and one such element was the extension of the interior beaten-earth floor beyond the entrance. This under-the-eaves area is re-created in the Shokatei; it is a shadowy space important for participants in their preparation for the tea ceremony. It provides a vital transition from the bright bustle of the world outside to the mellow-hued tranquillity inside the tea house.

Stone basins, stone lanterns, bridges, paths, houses and waiting pavilions — these elements all show the refined restraint associated with tea gardens, and a thorough attention to design and detail. The elegance of the residence is unsurpassed, with its unfinished wood structure, white walls and shingle bark roof. A platform was added to the Old Shoin for the purpose of viewing the moon rising over the garden, a delightful pastime for guests in the evening. The choice of rocks continues the overall sense of restraint, with some tall examples at certain places as accents to the composition.

The garden at Katsura was mostly constructed between 1620 and 1625 by Prince Tochihito. The designer is unknown, although the tea master Kobori Enshu was known to have been one of the prince's friends. Whoever the designer was, he skilfully blended the spirit of larger-scale Heian-style gardens with the tea garden, thereby creating a large garden with great beauty and repose. The result included so many unique techniques and developed so many styles of different elements that it inspired garden designers throughout the Edo period.

The under-the-eaves space at Shokatei tea house at Katsura, showing the shadowy transition area between the world outside and the inner world of tea.

Left: A view of the miniature Ama-no-hashidate sand spit in front of the Shokintei tea house at Katsura, with the bridge and lake in the background. This is a fine example of elements scaled down to size, giving the impression that the garden is limitless.

Below: A masterful miniature landscape at Katsura, with the essential ingredients of lake, hills and paths, as seen from the Shoin building. At no viewpoint can the whole garden be observed; at every turn and over every hill a new view is unfolded.

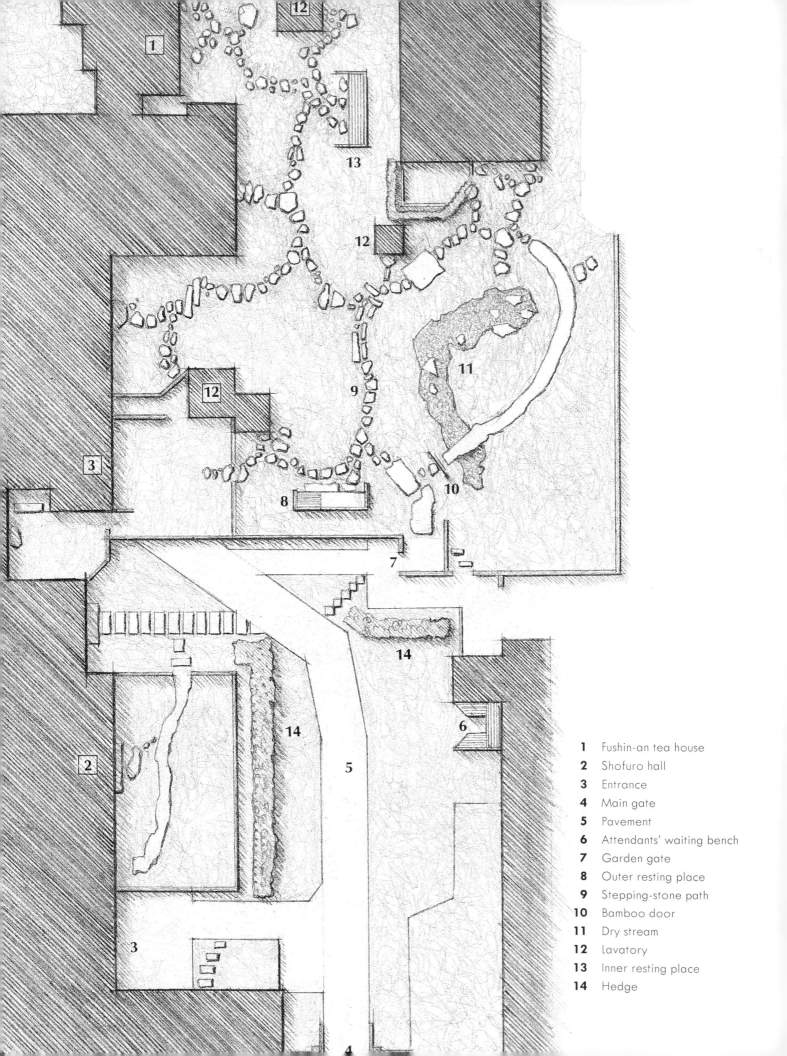

1   Fushin-an tea house

2   Shofuro hall

3   Entrance

4   Main gate

5   Pavement

6   Attendants' waiting bench

7   Garden gate

8   Outer resting place

9   Stepping-stone path

10   Bamboo door

11   Dry stream

12   Lavatory

13   Inner resting place

14   Hedge

Omote Senke

Omote Senke is one of the three schools of tea set up in Kyoto by the three grandsons of Sen no Rikyu. All the original buildings have burnt down and been rebuilt, but the gardens resemble the way they would have appeared in the seventeenth century.

The garden in which the Fushin-an tea house sits is divided into outer, middle and inner gardens. Guests pass through the garden gate (as shown opposite), treading on stepping stones, and assemble at the outer waiting bench. They then pass through a window gate, which is simply a section of clay wall with a protecting roof, pierced by a low window. Here guests have to humble themselves by stooping, and then pass through a further gateway into the inner garden. Each time they are symbolically moving away from the worldly exterior. The inner garden has another waiting bench and a curious old sand toilet which, incidentally, is not used now! Once under the eaves of the tea house, the guests step up through the small door into the 'world of tea'.

Left: Plan of Omote Senke, showing the gradual progression through gateways and along winding stepping-stone paths, symbolically moving away from the exterior world to the small doorway leading to the 'world of tea'.

The essence of 'an untrodden way' to a hermit's hut is achieved here at Omote Senke tea school by the careful placing of stepping stones, the moss floor covering and the natural appearance of the tea house.

Koho-an

Koho-an temple and the original Bosen tea room were designed by Kobori Enshu (1579–1647), a very talented Zen practitioner, tea master and garden designer. His choice of the name Koho-an is interesting: the first character (ko) means solitary or alone, the second (ho) means the thatched-roof covering seen on peasants' *sampans,* and the third (an) means retreat.

Enshu's original stone pavement runs for about 40 metres (44 yards) from the main entrance up to the front gate, with only one right-angled turn in its outer portion. Its severity is befitting a Zen temple, but the pedestrian is kept interested by the detail of the stones. Dressed (or cut) and natural stones are skilfully fitted together, in a similar way to the stone pavement on p.114.

Although Enshu's Bosen tea room was destroyed by fire, it was accurately reconstructed in the eighteenth century. It is unique in its design. The room is built in the Shoin style with paper *shoji,* or screens, filling the upper half of the opening that faces the garden (see opposite). Thus the view of the garden beyond is a horizontal composition, rather like a painting. In fact, the garden is said to have been inspired by 'Eight Views of the River Hsiang', which was a famous series of Chinese landscape paintings. The landscape in miniature uses stone lanterns, cobbles to represent the seashore, and limited planting. The *shoji* give the impression that the guests are afloat in a boat, which relates back to the second character in the name Koho-an. Guests enter the tea room through the low opening under the *shoji.*

Tea gardens introduced a number of important principles into garden design, and they embodied the philosophy of tea that was firmly embedded in both Japanese culture and the Japanese psyche. Rikyu had, by his aesthetic of simplicity and restraint, spread the 'way of tea' to the populace.

The introduction and development of designs for stone lanterns, water basins and stepping stones were very important to later gardens. Perhaps even more influential, tea gardens introduced the concept of an 'untrodden path' in a tightly enclosed space, such as is often found in the middle of a town or city, which had the effect of bringing the aesthetics of tea into people's lives.

A nobleman called Yamashima Tokitsunga wrote in 1529, after visiting the tea master Soju at his home, 'The tea house has the look of a small dwelling in the mountains. It expresses great feeling and must truly be called a quiet retreat in a city.'

During the Edo period, the tea garden became stylized through its use by the general populace. Often people could not fit a tea house into their property, so instead they brought the spirit of the tea garden into their courtyard, or *tsubo.* The compositions were made to be viewed from the interior of the house or from the verandah, and many fine examples still exist in Japan's cities.

The composition seen from inside the Bosen tea room at Koho-an is framed by the shoji *or paper screens. There are numerous associations with being in a boat passing close by the shore of a river.*

chapter 3

Design Principles

Before considering designing in a Japanese style it is essential to gain an understanding of the underlying principles involved. All these have become apparent as gardens have evolved over the centuries. Some historical gardens, as you will have read in Chapter 2, emphasized certain detailed ideas, whereas all embodied the general principles to which the Japanese adhered in creating gardens.

Many of these principles were laid down as rules in the *Sakuteiki* or Book of Garden, which was attributed to Tachibana-no-Toshitsuna in the eleventh century and handed down to garden-makers ever since. Its opening words laid down important guidelines:

In making the garden, you should first understand the overall principles.

1 According to the lay of the land, and depending upon the aspect of the water landscape, you should design each part of the garden tastefully, recalling your memories of how nature presented itself for each feature.

2 Study the examples of works left by past masters and, considering the desires of the owner of the garden, you should create a work of your own by exercising your tasteful sense.

3 Think over the famous places of scenic beauty throughout the land and by making it your own that which appeals to you most, design your garden with the mood of harmony, modelling after the general air of such places.

(Shigemaru Shimoyama)

The Japanese Garden in the Washington Park Arboretum, Seattle. The influence of Katsura can be seen in the lake and in the use of the miniature sand spit and lighthouse in the middle distance.

Enclosure

All Japanese gardens have enclosure, but the extent of it varies. It was explained in Chapter 1 that the mountainous topography of Japan meant that, of necessity, dwellings were close together and gardens tended to be small, often enclosed by neighbouring houses or boundary walls, or indeed by adjacent hillsides. However, even when gardens are open and large in area, enclosure is considered desirable and has to be created. The exception is when the *shakkei*, or 'borrowed scenery', principle is used, but this is described later.

There are many reasons why enclosure is desirable: it makes the garden into a private space with the potential for an atmosphere of quiet and calm; it creates an immediate division between the world of the city and the world of the garden, which reinforces the concept that the ordinary city scale does not apply to the garden; the enclosing element itself can act as a 'canvas' or background to the compositions and other elements in the garden. Above all, an enclosed garden seems essentially right when you consider the important influence of Zen gardens and tea gardens. This enclosure contrasts markedly with the spaciousness of the French gardens in the sixteenth and seventeenth centuries with their grand parterres and extending vistas. It also contrasts with the lack of enclosure around many Western-style houses. The Japanese consider it important to divide the front of the property from the back and to separate public from private space.

The type of enclosure is important and determines the character of the garden. A neutral background is preferred so that the enclosing element does not try to compete with the composition in front. The most important enclosing elements are those at the rear of the composition, at the point furthest from the viewer. Fences and screens are favoured because they can be made from natural rustic materials, showing the strong influence of tea gardens, but they should always be of a simple design. In general, fences are more important than in Western-style gardens because, apart from their practical function, they are aesthetic elements in themselves, to be appreciated as such by the viewer and not completely covered by planting. At a practical level you may find yourself stuck with a neighbour's fence that is aesthetically out of place, in which event you should consider putting up a screen fence in front of it. As a general rule, it should not be possible to see through screen fences except for bringing in a special view beyond the garden, and around the edge of the garden the fence should be above eye level.

There are places where partial enclosure is needed, either in an isolated position or at a low height. Single screens are sometimes placed behind a particularly important element, such as a water basin or specimen plant groups, to create a composition that is uncluttered by the elements behind. They are also used to screen off waste-bins or areas used for garden maintenance. Low fences are sometimes employed to define areas of different use in a garden or to help direct the movements of the users.

When viewing from inside the house or pavilion, elements integral to the building also enclose. The sky is an important element in Japanese gardens, and exposure to it needs to be carefully controlled to create a balanced composition. If there is too much sky then there is too much Yang, or positive energy, and not enough Yin, or negative energy, which in this case is earth. The eaves and verandah of the building, overhanging trees and picture windows all enclose the sky element and are used to help create the right balance.

You can also use a change in level or mounding to create enclosure. Japanese gardens are rarely completely flat, especially where plants are incorporated in the compositions. A level change can be created with a planted mound, natural rock wall, or timber stakes driven into the ground. In creating, for example, a suggestion of mountain scenery, the soil will be built up into a mound, probably with the use of rocks. Where there is a stream, either actual water or dry, the water will flow from high to lower ground and the soil will be mounded up to make this change of level. This in itself creates a degree of enclosure, especially when planted up.

Planting is a useful element, but is used in a different way from Western-style gardens. The Japanese rarely use trees for overhead enclosure in a small garden; the overhang of a building or a pergola would be more common. Tree trunks are, however, sometimes used for a framing function.

Trees in Japanese gardens tend to be species that do not grow too large, or they are kept small by pruning. Tall shrubs and hedges are often used for enclosure, for which evergreen, small-leaved types are preferred that blend in well as a background. These too would be frequently pruned in a small garden. As well as having an enclosing function, trees and shrubs have a screening function if a particular view is poor or a neighbouring property intrudes into the garden space.

The moss garden at Ryogen-in, Kyoto, uses the enclosing element of the plain tile-capped wall to good effect. The garden is usually viewed from the verandah on the right.

Viewpoints

The direction in which compositions in the garden are to be viewed is very important and is determined right at the beginning when a garden is planned. Japanese gardens contrast with Western-style gardens in that they are not designed for people to wander through in an unplanned way. Instead, the Japanese tend to look at their gardens from a limited number of viewpoints. In some of the paradise gardens and most of the Zen gardens, the viewpoint was a sitting position on the floor of the temple or pavilion. Even where people were encouraged to walk through the garden, as at Katsura Detached Palace and in tea gardens, the number of viewpoints was limited and controlled as one journeyed through the garden.

In the Japanese house, the view from the guest room is traditionally the most important and the garden tends to be designed around this. In a Western-style house, the lounge or dining room would probably be considered most important. It has to be decided if the garden is to be appreciated from a sitting or standing position, or from specific points as you walk through the garden. A large garden will need to be walked through to be appreciated, but it does not follow that a small garden is only viewed from the edge. Tea gardens are small, but can only be properly enjoyed by walking through them.

Viewpoints will also be affected if the principle of *shakkei* or 'borrowed scenery' is employed. The appreciation of scenery beyond the garden (which is being 'borrowed') will certainly be heightened from one particular viewpoint, which needs to be determined. After this the main garden composition can be proposed and located. Direction of view will influence the way the composition faces and the flow between compositions.

The shakkei *viewpoint from the top of the hill at Shugaku-in Villa, reached after a long climb with restricted views.*

This London office design uses rocks, pebbles, plants and a lantern to create balance in the traditional style.

Composition and Balance

A Japanese garden attempts to re-create the harmony and balance in nature. To achieve this one needs to spend time studying nature in the wild and to look at paintings to see how artists view the natural world. The idea is to experience nature in all ways and, in doing so, to absorb its essence, thereby obtaining some understanding of it. The way waterfalls relate to the hills behind, the way rocks are grouped to guide the water over the fall and the way the fall is broken at the bottom, the type of plants found near waterfalls and their patterns of growth, the way streams find their way through the landscape — these are some of the lessons to be learned.

The secret, however, is not slavishly to try to re-create such wonders of nature, but to look at them from an artistic viewpoint. Designers came to realize that by a process of simplification and refinement, the essence of a natural feature could be captured by a composition in a garden. The introduction of certain symbols was enough to spark off an association in the mind of the viewer; a single rock could become a mountain, a small mound a hillside, and an area of raked gravel a sea.

From this process of study and experience, a number of guidelines become clear. Each historical Japanese garden has a particular emphasis or theme, and any newly created garden also needs this. By reference to past garden types and styles, a theme can suggest a famous natural scene, as

was done in some early paradise gardens, or symbolize a part of wild nature such as lofty mountains, deep gorges, waterfalls, tumbling mountain streams, a slow-moving river, marshes or the sea, as was done in many of the Zen gardens. Alternatively, you may consider that a 'dewy path to a tea house' is the kind of atmosphere that you would like to create, as was done in the tea gardens.

Observation of nature also reveals the preference for asymmetry over symmetry, but with asymmetry always in a balanced state. By emulating this, Japanese gardens always seem to be harmonious and free of discord. The question is how to achieve balance without resorting to symmetry. Here the Japanese latched on to certain numbers and forms. First, elements are always grouped in odd numbers — threes, fives, sevens. Grouping gives continuity and an overall cohesiveness to a composition. Second, the form of the triangle is one that can be asymmetric and yet at the same time balanced, and as such is often used for groups of rocks or trees. However, the three elements in a triangle still need to be balanced in respect of the mass and weight.

Space is an important element in garden compositions in just the same way as it was significant in landscape paintings. In these, the spaces between the painted images help balance the composition and are the deep, mysterious elements that can only be grasped when the mind is allowed to wander. The Chinese philosopher Lao-tzu wrote:

'Though clay may be moulded into a vase, the essence of the vase is in the emptiness.' The spaces in gardens are the expanse of gravel or moss, the pond, the enclosing wall or the sky. They have a similar function to those in paintings and need to be the right size and shape to achieve the correct balance.

The scale of elements is also important. The height of elements can be chosen to give an illusion of perspective and distance, but they should never seem out of scale with their neighbour. If an element seems out of scale on its own, however, it can often be balanced by the introduction of another element. For example, at Entsu-ji the mass of the rock groups is balanced by the addition of planting (see p.84); at Tenryu-ji and Daisen-in a rock group is balanced by a bridge in front (see pp.45 and 51). Getting the scale right is easier with gardens in Japan, where plants tend to be planted at their mature height or at the height at which the designer planned that they be kept. If you are planting smaller, more standard nursery-stock sizes, then the plants should be at an equal state of immaturity to give you a composition in 'miniature' after construction, with the plants maturing with time. With rocks, scale is easier to achieve, as the rock can always be buried in the ground to reduce its size. Garden ornaments are more difficult to deal with, especially stone lanterns, which can be too big for a small garden. If you buy an ornament that is out of scale, try partially screening it with planting or a mound.

When designing a garden much will depend on your own outlook on life, your religion, your desires and aspirations. If a garden for contemplation and meditation is needed, then a *karesansui* may be right; if you seek a calming, serene influence, then a 'dewy path' could be appropriate. On the other hand, if you strive for more activity and sensual interest, perhaps waterfalls and a pond with fish in it would be more suitable. All these can be created by assembling in a composition elements that are cues symbolizing the natural feature. A Japanese garden, however, can never be just a collection of ornaments — a number of other design principles must be utilized in creating the composition.

The karesansui *at Taizo-in, a dry landscape garden of the Muromachi period, takes the process of simplification and refinement to the extreme with a well-balanced rock composition, moss and raked gravel. Space is used in an abstract and symbolic way.*

Contrast and Change

Japanese gardens are full of contrast and this is one reason why they have an immediate impact, even if the viewer's level of understanding of the design or appreciation of the underlying philosophy is small. There is contrast between the elements used — between plants and rocks, plants and gravel, plants and fences, water and rocks — in terms of colour, texture, form and indeed presence. Consider the different feeling you have when standing against rocks compared to standing by plants.

Among the different plant materials used, there are also differences in colour, texture and form, even with the predominance of evergreens — the low ground-hugging moss up against taller shrubs or bamboo up against trees. The designer tends to use a number of evergreen shrubs of one species, such as azalea, massed together, bringing continuity to the design. Then in sharp contrast a deciduous open-branched shrub or tree like *Acer palmatum* (Japanese maple) will be introduced, perhaps as a single specimen, but still very powerful. Much of this stems from the tea gardens, where the design was inspired by a 'dewy path' through a forest. Here various shades of green are encountered in moss, shrubs, trees and even lichen-covered rocks, until you suddenly meet a tree in full autumn glory.

Change comes in two main forms, first that which the viewer experiences as he moves through a garden, and second the change in seasons so celebrated by the Japanese. Gardens are rarely revealed to the viewer all at once. As viewpoints are very important and are decided upon at the beginning of a design, there are great opportunities to heighten the viewer's expectations, and the Japanese exploit this to the full. The garden at Katsura Detached Palace in Kyoto is perhaps the most perfect example. With every step, you get the feeling that your emotions are in the hands of the designer — viewpoints extend only as the designer wants them to and are cut off by a modest hill or clump of planting. Varying path types and surfaces lead up a hill, and then down to a bridge. At no time can you see the whole garden at once — something that Western gardens frequently allow. After walking around Katsura, it is astonishing to see from a plan just how small it really is, only 4 hectares (11 acres) in area, for it gives you a continual sense of expectancy and surprise.

At Shugaku-in Villa garden, near Kyoto, the entrance is through the Onarimon gate, and you travel up a sloping path with tall hedges on both sides, which restrict any view. The path goes up only about 10 m (33') in elevation, but the

One of the paths at Katsura, winding up a hill out of view and thus heightening the sense of expectancy in the visitor.

The changing seasons are highlighted by flowering trees. Rocks and planting contrast in colour, texture and form.

sense of expectancy enhanced by the lack of view makes it seem much higher. At the top the view is revealed, made all the more magnificent by the upward route (see p.74).

Even smaller gardens create a sense of change through expectancy and surprise. With the paramount importance of enclosure, small gardens around houses or temples tend to be divided up for different uses. Moving from one space to another through gateways, past screens and fences heightens the sense of anticipation. Gardens such as Daisen-in at Daitoku-ji Temple in Kyoto may appear as though they can be seen all at once, as there are few divisions in the design. However, the divisions are at a metaphysical level — from the *shoin*, or study, the eye is immediately attracted to the very powerful stone waterfall group with the stone bridge below. It then travels down the mountain 'stream' under the covered timber bridge and down the 'river' with the junk-shaped rock (see pp.17, 48–51).

The Japanese also manipulate to advantage changes in light. In passing through a building, shadowy corridors lead to bright courtyards where the natural light is increased by light-coloured gravel on the floor. The 'under-the-eaves' area of the tea house is important in the lengthy process of preparing the minds of the guests. It represents the transition from the relative brightness of the tea garden to the relative darkness of the tea house. In creating this contrast, the guest is prepared for the reduced light intensity in the tea house proper, and further sheds the distractions of the outside world as a preparation for the ceremony.

As part of their love and great reverence for nature, the Japanese celebrate the different seasons. The climate of Japan makes the seasons very marked and, set against a background of indigenous evergreens, the blossom in spring and the rich autumn colours have a dramatic impact. The cherry-viewing season is celebrated with parties, processions and a lot of *sake*-drinking. It is quite a sight to see large groups of families and friends sitting under the cherry blossom in the city's parks. As well as the obvious colour changes, more subtle ones are appreciated and designed into projects — for example, the bright green of the maple leaves as they break bud marking the beginning of the growing season, and the flowering of the azaleas in late spring signifying the beginning of summer.

Autumn colour spectacularly, but totally naturally, celebrates the changing of the seasons.

Perspective

In Chinese paintings the spaces between the elements in a composition are all-important. They tend to have three planes — foreground, middle distance and background — and the eye jumps from one plane to another across the spaces. Images in paintings either get larger or smaller as your eyes move from the viewpoint, and this is the same for Japanese gardens. With the popular desire to make the garden a microcosm of nature, the Japanese often wanted to create an illusion of distance and they achieved this by the positioning and manipulation of design features. A stream or path can be widened near the viewpoint, quickly getting narrower in the relative distance, or rocks can be large in the foreground and unusually small in the background. Heights and textures can also be manipulated. The foreground may have full-size trees, the background dwarfed ones; textures may be very coarse in the foreground and very fine in the background, again giving an illusion of distance. Coarse textures and forms might be a mature pine tree, whereas fine textures and forms might be clipped box or other small-leaved shrubs. Objects can be overlapped to give an illusion of perspective and therefore distance, as well as to heighten the sense of expectancy.

Where a feeling of spaciousness and distance is sought, ponds will be wider near the viewpoint and narrower further away. The presence of islands and land jutting out into the pond from the sides creates layers in a garden in a similar way to Chinese paintings and tends to increase its spaciousness. As well as elements getting smaller as they recede from the viewpoint, they can also get bigger, which has the effect of foreshortening distance. For instance, at Kinkaku-ji, the small pines on the island are perceived as full-size (see opposite), thus exaggerating the width of the pond. The stone lantern in the garden and the similar one on the hillside at Joju-in, Kyoto, (see p.86) give reference points to enable the viewer to perceive distance. The posts holding up the eaves on verandahs of traditional houses and temples also act as reference points, as does the verandah platform itself. The posts are either square-section timber or, in some tea houses, natural trunks, which give the effect of looking through a grove of trees.

The verandah platform also has an important effect on the evaluation of distance. As one looks out from such an elevated position, the ground immediately in front and below the platform is cut off from view. The effect is that the experience of the viewer is modified and the viewed object becomes more impressive. The garden composition tends to 'float' in space.

Right: The pines on the island at Kinkaku-ji are kept at the same size by constant pruning in order to maintain the illusion of distance and create perspective in relation to the pond.

Overleaf: At Tenryu-ji the land jutting out from the side of the pond creates the same effect as the layers in Chinese painting and increases the sense of space in the mind of the viewer.

Shakkei

The Japanese word *shakkei* literally means 'borrowed scenery', or 'borrowed landscape'. It is the principle whereby a view or element outside the garden is captured and brought into the garden as part of the composition. This should be distinguished from merely using an interesting or inspiring view as an incident in the garden. With *shakkei*, not only is the view used in the composition, but the garden is designed to develop the relationship between garden and view, so that the view becomes that much more poignant and effective.

The first essential element for *shakkei* is the landscape to be 'borrowed'. In Japan the most common landscape is mountains, although some designers have 'borrowed' waterfalls, woods, marshes or even interesting structures such as gateways and pagodas. In the West, as few of us have a mountain view from the garden, the technique can be extended to use a group of trees or even a single tree in a neighbouring garden. As with all Japanese techniques, the object is not to bring the whole landscape view into the garden, but only enough to suggest its essential spirit. There may be buildings between the garden and the landscape to be 'borrowed' that would detract from the composition. Therefore, just as an artist sometimes exercises licence in painting a picture, the landscape designer skilfully omits that which is superfluous and confusing.

Below: A classic example of shakkei *at Entsu-ji, where Mount Hiei (on the left in the far distance) is 'borrowed'. The clipped hedge behind the rocks provides the interface.*

Right: shakkei *at Shoden-ji. A very simple but stunning design with clipped bushes against a white wall, which serves to 'capture' Mount Hiei in the background.*

A wall or hedge, simple in design, with a well-defined horizontal top, serves both as an important division and as a link between garden and landscape in *shakkei*. It acts as a frame to the view beyond, an interface that the eye falls on without registering detail. It also conceals the ground between the wall or hedge and the view. All this limits one's ability to perceive distance and the eye leaps from the wall or hedge directly to the view. If the link is a wall, as at Shoden-ji, then it should be a plain textured one with simple coping. A hedge, as at Entsu-ji for example, should be a small-leaved evergreen species and clipped to give a level top. The other aspect that makes *shakkei* more than just a nice view is the composition on the garden side of the wall or hedge, which has a special relationship with the view and creates a linkage. If the view is of a mountain, then rocks may make up the composition; for a view of a wood, then planting may be used.

One of the best examples of *shakkei* is at Entsu-ji, Kyoto. The stone composition in the foreground, softened by moss, suggests hills and a flowing river. The clipped hedge behind physically divides the garden from the landscape of Mount Hiei beyond, but aesthetically it has a more important function. First, it is the lower part of the frame that 'borrows' Mount Hiei into the garden by divorcing the viewer from the distance and depth of the mountain. Second, it is a backdrop to the stone and moss composition that sets up a linkage between garden and mountain beyond. Tall cypress and pine trees beyond the hedge in the middle distance form the other parts of the frame and help to draw the mountain in. The overall garden composition seems beautifully balanced, although it is thought that the cypress and pine trees did not exist when the garden was designed.

Shoden-ji, probably created by Enshu, is also a *karesansui* with a bed of white gravel on which are clipped azalea and camellia shrubs grouped in threes, fives and sevens. A plain white wall with clay tile coping serves as the backdrop to the garden and as the lower frame to 'borrow' the trees and Mount Hiei beyond. The clipped bushes help to expand the link between garden and trees and mountain.

Shakkei has an interesting variation in the garden of Shugaku-in Villa, where the sky is used as a framing element. Here the garden is large, with the *shakkei* view from the tea house in the upper garden, which is revealed after a long climb with a restricted view (see p.74). The *shakkei* has a pond in the middle distance backed by the 'great hedge', and beyond the scenery to be 'borrowed' are mountains and tree-clad hills. This is especially appreciated in the autumn.

Joju-in is also an example of *shakkei*, but rather an unusual one. The garden adjacent to the *shoin* has a pond with a stone lantern on the small island in the middle, showing the influence of tea gardens on the design. To the rear of the garden is a low clipped hedge and beyond, in the background, a tree-clad hillside rising up and creating enclosure in the distance (see below). The clipped hedge in itself creates the lower frame for 'borrowing' the hillside beyond, but there is an added ingredient. Part of the way up the hillside, the designer placed another stone lantern, creating an immediate and very powerful linkage with the lantern on the island. In this way, the whole hillside is effectively 'borrowed' and creates a brilliant composition.

An intriguing example of shakkei *at Joju-in, where the whole hillside is borrowed by the linkage between the stone lantern in the garden and the one on the hillside (just visible above and to the right of the garden lantern).*

Miniaturization

Elements can take on a new meaning when a garden is considered as a microcosm of nature with scale suspended. A rock becomes a mountain, a mound becomes a hillside, a pond becomes an ocean, a shrub becomes a tree, moss becomes a forest. Creating natural scenes in miniature relies on the fact that the designer has been able to simplify and extract the essence of the natural scene and re-create it as a garden composition. It also relies very much on the viewer, the participant and user of the garden, and their state of mind when they enter the garden.

In Japan, many gardens are arranged so that you enter via a series of linked spaces. You may, for instance, enter a traditional Japanese inn by a lattice door, directly off the street pavement, with a granite path leading up to the front door of the inn. As you pass through the shady corridors, a courtyard garden appears first on the left, then on the right. Then at the end you enter a *tatami* (rush) mat room with the *shoji* (screen) opening out on to the timber verandah, and beyond a *karesansui* garden with rocks, gravel and a few selected plants, bounded by a clay wall. As you pass through the front door the noise of the city in the street recedes, and by the time you reach the rear garden the troubles and tensions of city life have also faded away. In such a state of mind, sitting on the *tatami* mats or timber verandah, sipping green tea from a hand-crafted bowl, and looking out on to the rocks, gravel and plants, your mind can easily perceive the composition as a mountain landscape. Thus, the miniaturization is created not only by the hand of the designer but also by the mind of the user.

In many ways miniaturization is easier with the *karesansui* garden, as the imagination has already been stirred to see the gravel as water, and it can more easily take the leap to seeing rocks as mountains. Also, *karesansui* creates a more contemplative atmosphere, free from the sound of real water, which can sometimes be distracting. In general, miniaturization is more potent when the user is seated, looking out on to the garden. Ryoan-ji must be one of the finest examples. Hanryabo Terren, a priest of Ryoan-ji, wrote in the fifteenth century that 'thirty thousand leagues should be compressed into a single foot'. At Katsura, however, miniaturization was successfully achieved for the strolling user — a brilliant design.

Above: The serenity of the small rear courtyard garden can only be properly appreciated while seated on the tatami *mats.*

Left: Close-up of a composition at Daitoku-ji in Kyoto, where the rock represents a mountain and the gravel a sea. The illusion is preserved by the pine, kept small by pruning.

chapter 4

Design Elements

The various elements that are needed to make up a garden or landscape in the Japanese style are mostly unique to Japan and have been used over the centuries in historical gardens. Probably the greatest influences have come from the Zen gardens – most notably the use of rocks and rock groupings – and the tea gardens, for paths and ornaments. As the elements are described you should refer back to Chapter 2 to remind yourself of the original use of a particular element in order to understand its significance.

The juxtaposition of bold and simple elements makes an important statement. Here at Daisen-in tiles, stone edging, raked gravel and gravel cones provide strong contrast.

Rocks

Rocks have been revered since ancient times. Prehistoric people used them to mark important sites, such as the stone circles of Stonehenge in Wiltshire and Callanish in the Western Isles of Scotland. Research has shown that certain currents can be measured in such rocks, indicating that they have a power beyond mere matter. In Japan, too, areas of ground were cleared in geometric shapes and stone circles erected. A typical example of these is the Shinto shrine at Ise, which has a rectangular sanctified precinct marked by a ground covering of white gravel stone. According to ancient Shinto beliefs, rocks were hollow, inhabited by spirits or gods, and were often sanctified by wrapping straw ropes around them.

The Japanese have always attached great importance to the use of rocks in their gardens, an attitude that still prevails in modern Japan. Hideyoshi, a Japanese ruler of the sixteenth century, apparently thought so much of a famous rock called the Fujito Stone that he moved it 'wrapped in silk, decorated with flowers and brought it to the garden with the music of flute, drums and the chanting of labourers' (Loraine Kuck, *The World of the Japanese Garden*). The unchanging nature of rock suggests a presence beyond the ephemeral quality of the world. As such, its existence in the garden provokes a powerful association with the wild and massive aspects of nature. Rocks are considered to form the 'skeleton' of a landscape, which in many ways is more important than the planting. This means that, when constructing a garden or a landscape, the rocks are placed in position before the plants.

Standing stones at Callanish in the Western Isles of Scotland show that Japan is not the only culture to revere rocks. Folklore suggests that these are petrified giants.

Selecting Rocks

As with all Japanese arts, the selection of rocks requires care and sensitivity. The most favoured rocks are old and weathered, ideally with growths of lichen or moss, while those with interesting shapes are also highly prized. Round or square rocks are not considered suitable, and any kind of dressed or cut stone is rarely used. Finding suitable rocks in Japan is relatively easy, as specialized merchants carry stocks specifically for landscape use. In the West, however, it is difficult to find weathered rocks, although newly quarried materials can be bought from some garden centres, nurseries and stone companies. But as the emphasis is on rocks for walling or rockeries, which are unsuitable for use in Japanese gardens, much of the rock available tends to be too small.

Tall Vertical

Low Vertical

Arching

Reclining

Flat

The Japanese prefer subdued colours, although striking veining can be prized in the right place. If you require large quantities of rock you may find yourself restricted to a single type located near the project. However, for small quantities, garden centres or nurseries frequently stock a number of different types. It is best to select a type of rock that is durable, reasonably angular, though not sharply so, and available in pieces as tall as their width and depth. Granite is obviously very durable, but many sandstones and limestones are also durable enough to be transported and will last many decades in a garden. The colour and texture of the rock type should not look too new, or at least should weather quickly.

The selection of individual rocks is not easy, but it is of paramount importance to choose each individual piece and not simply order a tonnage to be delivered. Wherever you choose rocks, be it in a garden centre or stone quarry, you should try to see as many faces of the rock as possible. You will probably be confronted by a large pile of rocks with a limited number of faces showing, giving you little chance to make the right choice. In this case, try to persuade the salesman to move the rock about so that you can see several of the faces.

Before making your choice, spend some time looking at rocks and rock groups in nature and observing how they sit in the ground. Also look at rocks in other Japanese gardens. This is best done 'in the flesh', but pictures are useful as a second best. Certain shapes of rock are easily fitted into a composition and some are not. Once you have looked at as many faces of the rocks as possible, try to imagine which could be the top and which the front face. Remember that rocks should be sunk into the ground by at least one-third their height to make them stable, for both practical and aesthetic reasons. Therefore part will not be visible, which is an opportunity to bury any less attractive aspect of the rock.

It is vital to bear the size of your garden in mind; there is no point trying to put 5-tonne rocks into a small garden when 1- or 2-tonne ones would be more in scale. To give you some indication of size to weight: a 5-tonne rock, if in the shape of a cube, would be approximately 1.2 × 1.2 × 1.2 metres (4' × 4' × 4'), while a 1-tonne rock would be approximately 0.75 × 0.75 × 0.75 metres (2' 6'' × 2' 6'' × 2' 6''). Remember that granite tends to be heavier than sandstone or limestone.

Old garden books tried to classify rocks according to their shape: tall vertical, low vertical, arching, reclining and flat. They also gave examples of rock groups of twos, threes and fives, where the rocks were balanced. It is worth looking at such books in order to understand the concept of 'balance' in terms of the rocks' relative position, their size and mass, but they should not be read as 'pattern books', because invariably the rocks chosen for a project will be a different shape from those illustrated.

The choice of rocks will also depend on the theme on which the composition is based. Rugged, angular rocks are suitable for suggesting lofty mountains, but not for a waterside where softer, more rounded specimens would be more appropriate. A dry waterfall is often represented by the *Sanzon*. This is a triangular group of three rocks symbolizing the Buddhist trinity, with one large vertical rock and two smaller ones to create the balance, as shown below (left). The dry waterfall rock at Tenryu-ji has striations vertically down its face, suggesting water movement. Such a grouping can be extended by interlinking triangles created with more rocks, thus giving five- or seven-rock groups. In some cases, one of the group is omitted and left to the imagination.

Sanzon *Rock Group*

Plan of Sanzon

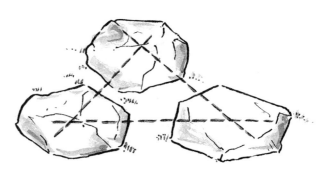

The Japanese garden in London's Holland Park, created in 1991, contains the classical elements of a waterfall set into a hill, balanced by the stone bridge spanning a pond.

Stone lanterns suggestive of a lighthouse complete the composition.
(Designer: Kyoto Garden Association)

Placing Rocks

On the placing of rocks, the *Sakuteiki* states:

There are many taboos concerning the placing of stones. It is said that if ever one of them is violated, the master of the house would constantly suffer from illness to the ultimate loss of his life and that the place would be deserted to become an abode of demons . . . Placing sideways the stone which was originally set vertically, or setting up vertically the stone which was originally laid sideways, is taboo. If this taboo is violated, the stone will surely become 'the stone of revengeful spirits' and will bring a curse.

(Shigemaru Shimoyana)

It is reasonably easy to avoid being cursed or having your garden become an abode of demons, provided that you keep various simple rules in mind! However, the words of the *Sakuteiki* are true to the extent that the incorrect placement of rocks will certainly bring its own curse as you try to lift and move them around. An individual rock naturally looks balanced if its outline seems to be heading away from its centre of gravity where it meets the soil (see below). This is achieved by selecting a suitably shaped rock, placing it the right way up and then setting it at least one-third into the ground. The rock should look as though it is spreading out below the ground. If the outline seems to be heading inwards, the rock tends to look unstable and therefore unnatural. If you cannot avoid an awkward junction, remember that planting can be used to disguise it. Check the rocks for strata and veining and make sure that they all flow in the same direction. It is very uncomfortable for the eye, and therefore unnatural, for distinct strata and veining to be going in different directions.

Something the *Sakuteiki* could not have described was the modern use of artificial rocks. The most popular artificial material is fibreglass, with the shape and colour modelled on real rocks, but artificial ones will always be an inferior product for a number of reasons. Close up it is obvious that they are not real rock. They do not weather to look old, but instead the colour is bleached out over the years by the sun, and they are not as durable as real rock — an important factor if used in a public place. Finally, they do not have the presence of rock, nor its properties suggesting a power beyond that of mere matter. Altogether, they are best avoided. If weight is a problem, for instance regarding the loadings for a roof garden, then it is better to design a garden without rocks rather than use artificial ones.

One cardinal rule is to select a variety of rock shapes for, after all, rocks in nature are always varied. If two rocks look similar, they should not be put near one another. Similar rocks bought for the same project can often be turned around the other way or left half-buried to make them look different. The *Sakuteiki* further advises:

If you place two rocks in front, you always have to follow them up with several others . . . Rock at the foothills or on plateaux should look like wild dogs staying low or wild boars running in all directions or small calves playing with their mother.

If you follow all these guidelines the rock, or rock group, once placed, should look as though it has been there for years. No other material gives such instant maturity to a landscape or garden.

Rocks should be sunk at least one-third into the ground. The left-hand rock looks balanced, whereas the right-hand rock is not set deep enough and looks unbalanced.

Water

Waterfalls and springs, like rocks and other natural elements, were seen in ancient Shinto beliefs as something to be worshipped. Of course, the importance of water is acknowledged the world over – by Christians in baptism, by Hindus for purification, and by Muslims for both purification and as a symbol of the flow of the life force. According to ancient Shinto custom, before worship one had to purify oneself with water – this would usually be presented as a waterfall, a stream or a water bowl for hand-washing and mouth-rinsing. In later years, water was considered essential in Pure Land Buddhism for paradise gardens; in these gardens people drifted on ponds in boats among the mystical isles and lotus flowers.

Water is a natural feature of the Japanese landscape: in the mountains there are many springs, waterfalls and streams, and lower down the slopes are wide-flowing rivers. Being a nation of islanders, the Japanese consider the sea very important and, even if not directly visible, its presence is highly significant. In Zen gardens, water was often symbolized rather than real but nevertheless was an essential natural element; in tea gardens, water was always present for washing and purification, usually in a water basin filled by a bamboo pipe.

Water has interesting and special properties: it takes on the shape of any vessel or container into which it is put, and it is present everywhere – in humans, animals, plants, in the soil and in the atmosphere. Like rocks, water is believed to be a powerful force, as evidenced, for example, by the practice of dowsing (water divining). If a dowsing rod passes over an underground stream, forces or currents will cause the rod to move.

Water brings both benefit and delight to any environment and gives constant motion to a composition. Its rushes, gurgles and splashes appeal to the sense of hearing; its reflections enhance whatever overhangs it; and its translucent properties seem to give an added dimension to whatever lies at the bottom. The presence of water is of practical advantage to the environment, as it cools the air in times of extreme heat and provides a level of insulation in times of extreme cold. On the coast, or where there is turbulent water over waterfalls, negative ions are given off, which are beneficial to our health and well-being.

The inter-connected ponds at Katsura, spanned by numerous bridges of different styles, bring life to the garden.

Design of Ponds

In Japanese gardens water moves only in a way that is totally natural. It can manifest itself in the form of ponds, streams and waterfalls, but never as a fountain. The nearest thing to a fountain in a Japanese garden would be a bubbling spring, or water falling from a bamboo pipe. The water is always kept moving and crystal clear, as a symbol of purity. The point of inflow into a pond, often a waterfall, is always made a visible element and a deliberate part of the design. Even slightly muddy banks are not tolerated and pools are usually edged with materials that keep clean, such as rocks, timber or cobbles.

Care and consideration must be taken when incorporating a pond into a garden design. Ponds should 'sit' well in the landscape and look as though they might always have been there. This is especially important in Japanese gardens, where the hand of nature needs to appear to predominate. It is important that the pond has a focal point, which is often a waterfall but could also be a bridge, island or hill. It should be at the distant end of a viewpoint, appearing to be inaccessible, and the whole pond should not be revealed from any one viewpoint.

The essence of a natural scene, such as this one in the uplands of Britain, could be introduced into a garden composition.

When designing the shape of a pond, nature should be the guiding principle. A number of ponds in historical gardens were shaped along the lines of the written character *kokoro*, meaning 'enlightened heart'; also popular were gourd-shaped ponds. It is important that the pond has an irregular flowing shape, with the larger body of water close to the viewpoint. Further from the viewpoint the body of water should diminish. If your design includes bridges, then the pond shoreline needs to accommodate these. Land jutting out from the side of a pond in the form of promontories and inlets increases the depth of the composition and makes sure that all is not revealed from one viewpoint. The pond at Tenryu-ji, as described in Chapter 2, is a good example of this.

Kokoro-shaped Pond

Gourd-shaped Pond

Islands

Islands can be of benefit to a pond and those such as the crane and turtle islands (described in Chapter 2) contribute symbolic meaning to a composition. Most commonly, islands are used to alter the view across a pond from differing points, concealing certain elements from one viewpoint only to reveal them at another. A waterfall is often the element that is screened in this way. Islands also serve as focal points and assist in increasing perspective, especially if they are planted up, for example, with pines – as at Kinkaku-ji (see Chapter 2). As a general rule, islands are best positioned near one shore and not in the middle of a pond. They can vary from a single rock to a substantial piece of land, and this usually depends on the overall theme of the pond. For instance, a tidal island could consist of partly submerged rocks with other rocks seen below the surface, whereas a coastal island might have a low profile ringed with rocks and some stunted pines.

A large island may be built up in profile, with rocks and small trees as you move further from the viewpoint in order to create an illusion of distance. Crane and turtle islands are easily made. Crane islands can consist purely of one 'wing' rock – an upright rock set on its edge on an island; low-lying 'head' and 'neck' rocks can then be added to give an impression of a crane in flight. For a turtle island the 'head' rock is the most important, being an oblong rock set at an angle; a similar, smaller rock is used to suggest the tail, and low rocks the legs. Instead of one or two isolated islands, a pond can have a chain of islets to emphasize a particular feature, or indeed to be a feature in themselves. At Saiho-ji, as described in Chapter 2, a chain of them suggests 'night-mooring stones'.

Josiah Conder's drawing shows two islands of different character connected by a monolithic stone-slab bridge. From Landscape Gardening in Japan.

Edging Ponds

The edges of the pond are an integral part of the design and the choices available are influenced by the type of construction proposed. This is explained more fully in Chapter 5. A gentle sloping bank can be covered in pebbles below the water line or can be planted with reeds, rushes and irises. The pebbles should be water-worn and light in colour so that they can be seen on the bottom through the shallow water. For steeper-edged ponds, rocks are more suitable as edging, preferably ones large enough to extend well below water level to give an illusion of depth, which is particularly important for islands. Alternatively, timber stakes can be driven into the ground with the soil at the back flush to their tops. Again, take a lesson from nature and see how cliffs on a shore-line, suggested by rocks, gradually give way to beaches, suggested by pebbles. All of this gives variety and interest to the shore-line of a pond.

Fish

Fish can be a colourful addition to a pond, and they are useful where a lot of movement and interest are desired. Koi carp are an obvious choice for a Japanese garden. They can be bought in a variety of colours and stages of maturity — from 75mm (3″) up to 750mm (2′ 6″) — and have great character. They can become very tame: I was once given bread by a Zen priest in a temple in Japan in order to feed his pet Koi in the temple's pond. The tame Koi not only took the bread from my fingers, but also sucked them in the process! It is, however, important to feed them regularly with proper fish food (about once a day), although Koi can live quite happily for a couple of days without food.

There are a number of factors to be considered if you plan to keep fish; the depth of the water, for example, is of primary importance. If the pond is outdoors, then a depth of at least 900mm (3′) is required in one area of it so that the fish can lie there during the extremes of cold weather. The larger the fish, the greater the depth needs to be. Do not, however, make the whole pond 900mm deep or your views of the fish will be restricted. If the pond is indoors then 600mm (2′) is a good average depth.

The type of fish will have a bearing on your choice of plants. Koi, for example, can be particularly destructive towards plants, and only tough reeds or rushes should be considered in areas that the fish can reach. Finally, the filtration system needs to be able to cope with the added problem of fish detritus and possible algal build-up, and the water should be tested to ensure the absence of chemicals before the fish are introduced.

Waterfalls

Waterfalls occur naturally at both the inlet and outlet of a lake or pond, and at intervals along stream courses when the water needs to change level. The waterfall is an important element of a pond, as the source of water needs to be visible in a composition and provides a vital focus. When positioning a waterfall, or series of falls, the various viewpoints from which it will be seen need to be taken into account to avoid interrupting the view, and the waterfall can then be angled to enhance a particular aspect. You may, on the other hand, choose to hide the waterfall by an island or planting, to reveal it from another viewpoint, thereby increasing the surprise. Waterfalls bring water to life by their ever-changing display of splashing and gurgling, but these sounds must be integrated into the design. The sound can be distracting or disturbing for a contemplative space or if it is close to a bedroom.

In nature, waterfalls come in a variety of shapes and sizes: there are the ones where a large volume of water falls from a great height in one drop; there are tall waterfalls which are broken up into several falls; and there are ones which have just a small volume of water dropping a short distance, creating a mere trickle. Water effects vary with the time of year, giving very fierce, turbulent water during the winter rains and a more gentle effect during summer droughts. Such changes in a garden waterfall are possible if a natural water source is available, but they are difficult to achieve with a re-circulated pump system.

By studying waterfalls in nature, designers tried in the past to classify types of fall and identify their elements to make them comprehensible to students of the art. Thus they listed 'single falls' and 'broken falls', and the broken falls category was sub-divided into 'two-step' and 'three-step' falls (see below). The ways in which water falls over the top of a weir were described as 'smooth falls' and 'uneven falls', and the effect at the base of the fall of the water-dividing stone was noted — it breaks the flow of the water falling from the top, making a splashing sound, and the increased droplets create added reflectiveness. Each type of waterfall has a different sound and overall effect in the garden. Consider, for example, the contrast of water falling directly from a height into a deep pool and one falling from a height on to rocks or pebbles.

Single Fall *Two-step Broken Fall* *Three-step Broken Fall*

The *Sakuteiki*'s advice on creating waterfalls was as follows:

. . . you must first select the Water Falling Stone (mizuochi-no-ishi). *This stone will look uninteresting if its surface is smooth like a cut stone. When the waterfall is as high as three or four feet, a mountain rock with distinct creased face and smooth lip should be used for the falling of water. However, such a stone may be found useless unless it goes well with the side stones* (wakiishi) *to be set on both sides of it. After setting the well-qualified Water Falling Stone in its place, and compacting the bottom without slightly moving the stone, the side stones should be installed. Then the opening between the Water Falling Stone and each of the side stones should be filled from the bottom to the top, no matter how high it may be, by ample applications of water-softened clay. Then the narrow spaces still left between the stones should be filled even using ordinary soil, and compacted by ramming.*

The water-falling stone or rock is particularly important, as its front face will be on view and its top will form the lip of the fall. This lip determines how the water will fall — whether it will be smooth or uneven, and whether the water will fall away freely from the water-falling stone or trickle down its face. The volume of water present is an important factor in determining this, and the depth required over the lip dictates the capacity of the pump — assuming a re-circulated system is being used. It is best if a small pool is created at the top behind the lip to make sure of a constant, even flow of water.

The side stones give the waterfall visual stability and contain the water as it descends; they are often at a slightly higher level than the water-falling stone. Other rocks are used to give either visual or physical support to the main rocks. The basin at the bottom of a fall tends to be broad, edged with rocks, and possibly with rocks under the water; or other symbolic references can be introduced, such as the 'carp stone' at the bottom of the waterfall at Kinkaku-ji (mentioned in Chapter 2). The detailed positioning of the rocks will be dealt with in Chapter 5.

Smooth Fall

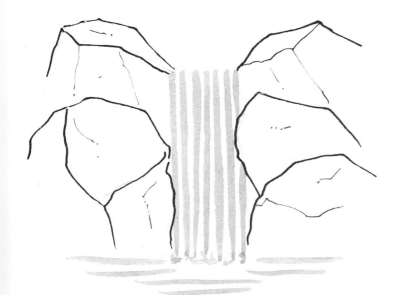

Uneven Fall

Streams

Although ponds bring water into a garden, that water is brought to life by the movement of the streams and waterfalls. The murmuring sound of a stream is particularly pleasing to the ear and at the same time does not disrupt a contemplative or meditative space. Paradise gardens of Shinden-style mansions frequently had streams leading under pavilions and covered passageways to link the house and the garden. These streams had to run in certain directions to accord with geomantic principles. The accepted layout was to have the main gardens facing south, and the *Sakuteiki* explains both this and the principles of stream design:

> The normal flow of the stream should start from the east toward the south, and then toward the west ... The most auspicious way is to let the stream start from the east side, come through under the building, and there flow through the south-east direction ... [it] should be made in some interesting and natural manner without the air of artificiality, the channel being dug touching this corner and that, this hillside and that, as the need and fancy call for.

As few of us have a natural stream flowing through our gardens, the stream will begin where it is designed to begin and will be re-circulated by a pump back to the start once it has travelled its course. It is possible to take a stream close to the house if both stream and house are adequately waterproofed. It is, of course, much easier to wind it through a pavilion or traditional-type timber platform built on legs.

Streams can be used to create an illusion of depth by narrowing quickly as they recede from view, as was explained in Chapter 3. The width of a stream can be varied according to the volume of water available — whether naturally or from the pump of a re-circulated system. What is a mere trickle at 300mm (1') wide with a small volume of water can become a torrent when 1 metre (3' 4'') wide with a large volume. A small stream is more effective when it can be seen moving over something, so consider placing gravel or cobbles on the stream bed. Generally, a stream should be kept fairly shallow, but the rate of flow can always be increased over a short stretch by placing rocks in the middle of it, which has the added effect of creating turbulence and a rushing sound.

Having taken the advice of the *Sakuteiki* and caused the stream to meander in a naturalistic way, you will need to introduce rocks if you wish to suggest an upland stream. Again the *Sakuteiki* has some advice:

> The placing of stones for the garden stream should start at a place where it makes a turn and flows along. This turn is supposed to have been caused by the presence of the rock, which the stream should not demolish. The stream after the turn flows with added momentum and hits hard against the object it encounters. That is the place where you will place the flow-round stone.

The practical reason for placing rocks at bends is to prevent earth from being washed away, and they do look natural in this position. The rocks should, however, be sunk well into the bank. Again, observation of streams in nature provides a wealth of lessons.

Left: A good example of a two-step waterfall in an early twentieth-century private garden at Cottered in Britain, giving the strong impression of a mountainous area behind. The rock to the left is particularly attractive.

Below: Blossom floating in a stream creates an unexpected event and delights the observer.

Dry Water

For the *karesansui*, or 'dry landscape', water is not actually present but is symbolized. There are a number of reasons why dry water is preferred to real water, reasons both philosophical — a dry landscape represents a developed abstraction that was perfected in the Zen gardens (already described in Chapter 2) — and practical — real water may be too difficult or too costly to include. Whatever the reasons, a dry landscape garden must be well designed to be successful and in many ways is more difficult to design than a garden using real water.

Many of the points previously made about water apply to dry water, as the concept of water is still present in the garden, although symbolized rather than actual. The dry landscape should be designed as though water were present, except that the basic principle of all Japanese gardens — of looking at nature and simplifying it to its basic essence in the garden — is taken one step further. For

example, a dry waterfall may be a single stone set at ground level rather than a series of stones set into the side of a hillock, as with a wet waterfall. Again, the dry landscape garden should only do with water that which is natural for it. Points of inlet and outlet need to be visible, viewpoints and a focal point in the composition should be considered. The shape of the pond has to be designed — whether like the written character *kokoro*, gourd-shaped, or a flowing irregular shape. Islands can be pieces of land but are more often represented simply by a rock set very low.

Gravel and Pebbles

To symbolize water you should use either small water-worn pebbles or sand. This is not, however, ordinary beach sand but a crushed granite or gravel, usually an off-white to grey colour, sometimes flecked with brown or red specks. In

Rock groups with strong vertical accents in a horizontal sea of gravel at Tofuku-ji temple.

Japan they use the deposits of gravel that accumulate at the bottom of cliffs as a result of erosion or weathering; in the West similar gravel can be obtained from a number of nurseries, garden centres and stone merchants.

Areas of sand or gravel in a garden are the equivalent of the spaces that are so important in landscape painting — mysterious elements that allow the mind to wander. The gravel represents a body of water such as a pond or the sea, and also streams or rivers. Using a wooden rake in a wavy, swirling motion, patterns are often raked into the gravel to suggest the movement of water with ripples and waves. There are good examples of this at Ryoan-ji and Daisen-in. When raking a water pattern into gravel, bear in mind that the top level of gravel represents the water level and that when it comes up against rocks, care needs to be taken to make it look convincing.

As gravel is not very durable it needs to be protected from the wind, contained by timber stakes or rocks, and should not be used where it will frequently be walked on. It is also advisable to avoid having an area of gravel near a lawn, as the granite chips can get into a lawn mower. A raked gravel design lasts for a couple of weeks before rain beats it down and it needs to be re-raked. Monks living in temples looked on this job of raking as a meditative exercise. Gravel is particularly useful in courtyards as it reflects light. It also provides a contrast to rocks and plants, and helps to make a composition vivid.

Water-worn pebbles can be used to suggest upland streams or rivers. These, again, should be an off-white to grey colour in order to suggest the bright reflective properties of real water, but the presence of a few red or black pebbles will add interest. Both gravel and pebbles look superb after rain, and the Japanese often spray them to bring out their beauty.

A bold composition using substantial gravel cones making an abstract statement at Komowake Ikazuchi Shrine.

Dry Waterfalls

If every element in a pond garden needs to be selected with great care and sensitivity, then in a dry landscape that care must be doubled. As water is such a powerful element in itself, it tends to draw attention away from other elements such as rocks, but without water all the elements are equally in focus. In a waterfall group the water-falling stone is crucial to the composition: it needs to be a vertical stone with a flat face at the front and, ideally, a slight indentation in the top to suggest where the 'water' flows over it. A stone with striations down the face of it, suggesting falling water, is particularly prized for this position. There is such a stone to the rear of the main pond at Tenryu-ji (see p.44); although dry now, it is thought originally to have been a waterfall with real water.

The principle of a dry garden is that even if the viewer does not imagine there to be water in the stream or river bed, the gravel or pebbles make it look as though water used to run there but has dried up, suggesting that it will run again after rain. The rocks in a dry waterfall seem to imply that the water might start to fall at any moment.

If there is a garden which brings out the true essence of Japanese religion and culture then it is the dry garden, for there the important influence of Zen, which is so especially Japanese, is embodied. In 1466, the poet priest Shinzui visited such a dry garden and wrote, 'The distant peaks and rushing streams nearby were altogether marvellous – so absorbing, indeed, that I suddenly lost all thought of returning home!' (Kinsaku Nakane, *Kyoto Gardens.*)

Left: A dry water course composed of water-worn cobbles flows from a symbolic waterfall in an office courtyard. A Japanese maple and waterside planting enhance the picture, which is designed to be viewed from the glazed corridor or from above.

Right: The severe but elegant lines of this garden are effectively displayed in the snow. The stone bridge is substantial but fits well into the large scale of the garden, and is set off by the tall lantern behind.

Bridges

Bridges have a number of functions. On a practical level they are there to take people across a body of water — be it real or dry — but they are also important aesthetically, drawing the eye across the water from one piece of land to another to create a link. They provide a focus, open up viewpoints and add a sense of stability and repose. At Tenryu-ji and Daisen-in, for example, a stone bridge in front of a waterfall group serves to balance the rock peaks behind, bringing harmony to the composition.

The style of bridge you choose depends on what type of stream or body of water it is to span and its proposed function. A heavy stone or timber bridge with substantial members would be suitable for crossing a rushing mountain stream, whereas a more delicate timber, stone or turf bridge may be used to cross a gentle brook. Some bridges are purely decorative and not intended to be actually walked on, but all bridges must be built to take the weight of an adult or child in case they insist on trying it out. As a general rule, a bridge should not only give support but be seen to give support, otherwise the eye will see that there is something awkward and false about it.

If people are actually going to cross at the bridge, the choice of style also depends on the response you want from them. For instance, if you want the user to linger at nearly every step you could try a stepping-stone bridge, as at the Heian Shrine, or a *yatsuhashi* plank bridge. To provide a quick, secure crossing a stone slab is effective, whereas a turf bridge warrants a pause and closer inspection. As a point of interest, *yatsuhashi* plank bridges were originally used to cross marshes on Japanese farms,

and were first brought into gardens in the Edo period.

A stone bridge can be of single or twin spans. A single-span bridge may be made of a simple piece of natural flat stone, whereas a twin-span one really needs two flat stones, reasonably well matched. Stones that arch are even better but are difficult to find. You can use dressed or cut stone but that gives a less rustic, more urban feel to a composition. You should be able to find suitable pieces from stone companies or sometimes from nurseries.

Any bridge needs to appear stable and well-anchored, and for this reason bridge-supporting rocks are set at each corner. These rocks are always substantial and are sunk into the ground so that only the upper part is seen. They can either be of equal height above ground level or the two on the side away from the viewpoint can be higher. These rocks balance the bulk of the bridge visually and provide a base from which the bridge springs across the gap.

The choice of bridge will often relate to other materials in the garden. If a lot of stone has been used, then a stone bridge would give continuity, but if timber predominates then a timber bridge will probably be more suitable. The log bridge at Saiho-ji (as shown on p.36) looks particularly appropriate in the mossy wood surrounding it. The answer is to go out and have a good look around your locality, bearing in mind that any bridge must be kept in scale with the rest of the composition. It is better not to have a bridge at all than to have one that ruins the overall composition.

Log Bridge

Turf Bridge

Single-span Stone Bridge

Twin-span Stone Bridge

Hills

As already emphasized, Japanese gardens are rarely completely flat. The Japanese have such a high regard for mountains that they are frequently symbolized in their gardens, for example by the use of earth mounds. These create a backdrop to a composition, which can then be planted up. The earth mound is also used to create the difference in level required for a waterfall; the rocks of the fall sit back into the mound, making it all look totally natural. Rocks, not connected with a waterfall, are sometimes set into a mound in order to suggest a crag or outcrop of rock on a hillside.

The *Tsukiyama*, or Artificial Hill Garden, was classified in the Edo period and fully explained by Josiah Conder in his

book published in 1893. It contains either one hill, a group of two or three, or sometimes hills in the form of a mountain ridge. They are usually combined with a pond or stream, the hills forming the background, with the pond or stream in the foreground. The pond often has a rocky island amid it with perhaps a pine trained in a twisted fashion, or maybe two crane and turtle islands.

The other main types of garden that were classified in the Edo period were the Flat Garden and the Tea Garden. Such classification is helpful for understanding the techniques used, but it should not be interpreted as a set of rules to follow. To merely copy the different styles described leads to stereotypes.

A Garden of 'Limitless View' drawn by Josiah Conder, showing his idea of the variety that can be achieved by the use of contours, bridges, lanterns, rocks and perspective.

Verandahs

Traditionally the verandah is part of a temple, tea house or dwelling house and is an important interface between building and garden. The verandah is an extension of the building, yet it is definitely considered to be 'outside'. It is part of the 'under-the-eaves' area that was so celebrated in tea houses as a preparation for the guest before entering the tea ceremony.

The traditional verandah is an elevated platform, sometimes with a rail around the edge; it is made of timber boards, which are usually stained a dark colour and

polished. Being partially protected from the elements by the extended eaves of the typical Japanese building, it is an ideal place from which to view the garden from a seated position.

Additionally it has a more aesthetic function when one is seated in the *shoin* or study. Together with the eaves and the posts holding up the eaves, the verandah acts as a framing or reference line, enabling the viewer to perceive distance in the garden beyond. It is also an enclosing element helping to create a balanced composition.

A verandah at Ryoan-ji temple provides a viewing platform for the garden. The eaves and support posts give a useful frame to the view.

Paths

In a Japanese garden, paths have a function beyond merely moving the user from place to place without getting muddy. They are intended to direct movement around the garden to some degree, but a more important purpose is to direct the user's senses and mind. In fact, some paths in a Japanese garden are never walked on except to gain access for garden maintenance. This contrasts markedly with most Western gardens, where paths invariably have a more practical function.

Design

In a practical sense, paths in a Japanese garden direct the user's movement from one viewpoint to another. The path in between may be in a cutting or screened off by planting so that views from it are limited, thus giving a marked contrast between the viewpoints and heightening the sense of surprise. In this way, the path not only directs physical movement but also the senses.

The curve or straight character of a path can be manipulated to great effect. A straight path will take the eye along its length to the end, and then draw the viewer to walk along its length to the end of the path. The Japanese often place an important object at the end of a straight path, such as an entrance to a building or a particularly beautiful water basin. A curved path will take the eye only as far as it can see before it bends; then, as the path curves round, a new vista is revealed.

Paths are a means through which a designer can link elements in a composition, thus directing the movement of the eye around the garden. In many historical gardens, with the observer seated in the *shoin*, looking out at the garden, stepping-stone paths lead the eye in a set route through the composition. Such paths create flow in the garden and ensure that the composition is appreciated as the designer intended.

The width of paths is a consideration not to be neglected. Not only can the width be adjusted to exaggerate perspective — by widening it near a viewpoint and then narrowing it as it recedes into the distance — it can also be used to direct the observer's movement. If a narrow path is allowed to broaden out locally, it encourages one to linger at that point and enjoy the view. This local widening is also useful at junctions where people need to stop before deciding which way to go. Stepping-stone paths should always have a larger stone at the junction of paths for this purpose.

Natural Stepping Stones   *Cut Stepping Stones*   *Stone Pavement*   *Two Stone Group*

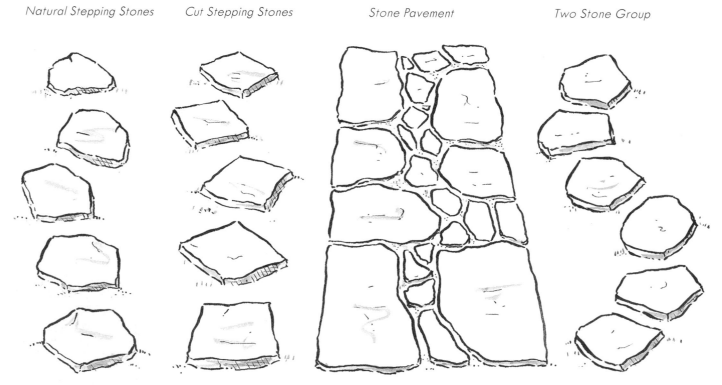

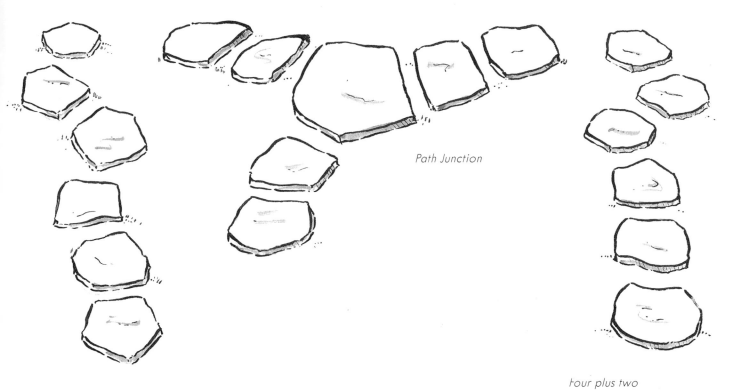

Path Junction

four plus two

Three plus two

Chidori or Zig-Zag

Ganko or Wild Geese

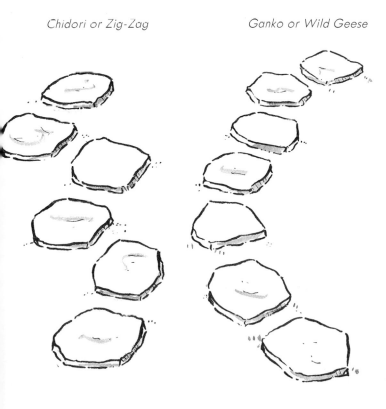

Some stepping stones are practical, some are purely ornamental. These at Konchi-in may never be walked on.

Materials

This brings us on to materials. Paths can be made from anything from beaten earth to bark, gravel, timber or stone. Stone paths (as shown below and opposite) can be of various types: either cut (or dressed) stone, individual natural stones, or stones fitted together to give a straight-sided path. A beaten earth or bark path suggests a route through woodlands or mountains, whereas a more regular stone path has an urban feel. One reason for this is that stone paths tend to be designed to be appreciated for themselves, whereas other path types are designed with the conscious decision to make them blend in with their surroundings.

As explained in Chapter 2, the use of stepping stones was developed in tea gardens to make the approach to the tea house both practical and aesthetic. Sen no Rikyu, the great tea master, is quoted as saying that stepping stones should be 60 per cent practical and 40 per cent aesthetic. They are easily accommodated in most types of garden composition, as they are very informal and fit in with a natural scene.

To an untrained eye, stepping stones in a Japanese garden often look thin and flat. This is in fact rarely the case, as one of the most important things about a stepping stone is its stability. When you step on the stone it must not

tilt, as this would give a feeling of unease. It is difficult to achieve this stability using thin, flat stones unless they are very large, therefore stepping stones are normally rounded rocks with one face flat and the rounded part sunk into the ground.

The size of the stones you use should vary according to the scale of the garden. In a small garden or enclosed area, 300 to 600mm (1' to 2') diameter stones are suitable, whereas in a large garden appropriate stones might be as large as 1,200 to 1,500mm (4' to 5'). Where a path meets a verandah a much larger stone called the *katsunugi-ishi*, or 'shoe-removing stone', is placed. The size of this stone is determined by the size of the other stones and the scale of the building or verandah.

As with a number of other Japanese gardens, the different designs of stepping-stone paths have been classified, the list being as follows: two stone groups, three plus two stone groups, *ganko* or wild geese, and *chidori* or zigzag. Good design sense can be achieved by studying historical gardens. As a rule, stepping stones are arranged in an alternating pattern which corresponds to the natural movement of the feet. The paths should branch out from a verandah, pavilion or house door, always avoiding cross-joints. The most important point to remember is that the

This long- and short-stone arrangement provides a natural-looking path rich in form and texture.

Although asymmetry normally prevails, a symmetrical layout here leads up to a bridge at Katsura.

stone should not be laid in straight lines. They should be 75 to 100mm (3" to 4") apart, to make them easy for everyone to walk on. Apparently, if laid further apart, women find difficulty walking on them, especially if they are clad in kimono and clogs! Where one stone face meets the next, the face chosen should be relatively straight, and the straight lines of adjacent stones approximately parallel.

The *garanseki*, or foundation stone, is placed where paths divide and is a larger stone to act as a visual balancing element. Traditionally a special stone is used as the *garanseki*, perhaps one from an old temple. In the West old temple stones are obviously not easy to come by, but you may consider using an old millstone. Such a large stone can also be placed where the path changes direction, or to emphasize an interesting ornament or other artefact. In the tea garden of the Yabonouchi School in Kyoto a large stepping stone is placed in front of an interesting length of bark from a much-loved but deceased tree.

Stepping stones do not have to be in natural stone, and dressed stone has been used in a number of historical gardens. You can use either square stones set on the diagonal, as at Katsura (see opposite, right), or long slabs of dressed stone; both provide an interesting contrast to the other natural shapes. Bear in mind, too, that whether

stones are natural or dressed they do not have to stop at marshes, streams or ponds, but can just carry on through them.

The transition between the asymmetry of the garden and the house or buildings can be effected by straight stone pavements. They may be used to provide a direct axial route to the main door of the house, and they can also be a helpful dividing element if one part of the garden has a Japanese theme and the rest is grass in the Western style. A favourite design for stone pavements is natural flagstones with an infill of cobbles — the cobbles break up the geometric lines of the path and provide a variation in colour and texture. Old reclaimed flagstones with one straight side are ideal and are normally cheaper than new stones, but a number of other materials can be used — even bricks laid in a basket weave or herringbone pattern are in sympathy with Japanese aesthetics.

Gravel and bark are most suitable for informal paths. Gravel has been used for centuries in temple gardens and is a cheap material that is easily integrated into natural surroundings. It does, however, need to be edged — for example with timber — to prevent it from spreading. Bark has not traditionally been used in Japanese gardens but is in sympathy with Japanese aesthetics and is perfect for creating the atmosphere of a path through a wood.

A stepping-stone path at Katsura with larger stones interposed at the path junctions

A random stone path of well-weathered and varied stones, set off well by the moss surround.

Lanterns

For many people the introduction of an ornament makes a garden truly Japanese, and unfortunately this misconception is perpetuated by many designers who have little knowledge of Japanese garden design. Typical ornaments to be found in a Japanese garden are lanterns, water basins, *stupas*, Buddhas and *shishi-odoshi*, or bamboo strikers. In fact, the term 'ornament' is misleading, as originally most had a practical purpose and became primarily aesthetic only as gardens developed.

There are traditional gardens in Japan that do not have a single stone lantern or water basin, yet they are every bit a Japanese garden. Ornaments need to be selected with great care and sensitivity and should be used with restraint, so as not to detract from the naturalism of the composition. At the same time they are a useful tool for developing a certain atmosphere, they can be used as a focal point or to create an illusion of distance and, of course, their practical functions bring elements such as light and water into a garden.

Stone lanterns were first introduced into gardens by the tea masters. As tea ceremonies often occurred in the evening, light was needed to show the guests the way through the garden. Sen no Rikyu particularly liked them because the gentle light given out by the tallow candle created the right atmosphere for the tea ceremony.

The design of these tea gardens was based on early hanging temple lanterns, which were made of bronze. Before Rikyu, stone lanterns were rather ornate and named after the shrine or temple where they originated, such as *Kasuga*-style and *Nigatsudokata*-style. After Rikyu, other styles were developed by the tea masters which were less ornate, for example *Rikyu*, *Oribe* and *Enshu* (see below). Some lanterns were named after their shape rather than their designer – thus we have *yukimo-doro*, or the snow-viewing lantern, so named because of the subtle way in which snow is held on the roof. They are frequently used near water and their squat shape makes them easy to fit into a composition (see below, right). Katsura is the best place to view lanterns, as it has no fewer than twenty-four, all with different characteristics: some are short, some tall, some square, round or hexagonal, some with pedestals and some without.

The Japanese favour old stone lanterns that are well-weathered and a premium is paid for such pieces. In the West we mostly have to make do with new ones and, even then, only a limited number of real stone ones are imported from the Far East. Reconstituted stone lanterns are manufactured in the West and are available in a few different styles, but how well these weather depends on the constituents. Although cheaper than real stone, they are inferior to the discerning eye. The really inferior ones, however, are those made from concrete and synthetic resins, which never weather to an old look and are best left out of the garden.

Even though lanterns are now included mainly for aesthetic reasons, they should be placed in the garden as

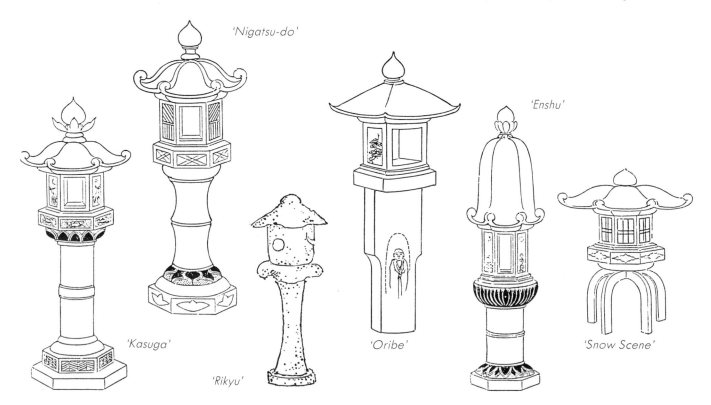

'Nigatsu-do'

'Enshu'

'Kasuga'

'Oribe'

'Snow Scene'

'Rikyu'

though they were still being used for light; only then will the lantern be in the right place. Suitable positions are at path junctions, the base of a hill, the edge of a pond or stream, near a bridge or a water basin. As the candles were originally lit by hand, a minimum of two stones was needed around a lantern — one to stand on, and another to place the candle container on. A large flat rock should be placed in front of the lantern for standing on, and a slightly taller, flat-topped rock placed to the side, ostensibly for the candle container. The arrangement is thus trianglar, and the size of the rocks chosen creates the necessary balance with the lantern. Sometimes a group of evergreen bushes or a tree is placed behind a lantern, with a branch gracefully hanging over it.

When choosing a lantern, bear in mind the scale of the lantern and the size of your garden. The type of lantern that has a large pedestal, for example, is very difficult to fit into a small garden or courtyard. As a general rule, simple designs will fit in with most compositions; near water try a more squat-shaped lantern.

Unless you are designing a large area it is best to use just a few lanterns. One or two will provide illumination at night. The face of the flame box should be turned towards the object to be lit, be it a water basin, a particularly good rock group or a bridge. A candle is the most harmonious light form, preferably protected by paper panels or, as second best, frosted glass. Electric light tends not to be subtle enough, and also adds the complication of wiring up.

Below: Stones were originally set around a lantern for the purpose of tending it.
Bottom: A family of stone lanterns at Tochogu, Nikko.

Water Basins

Water basins originated, in a similar way to lanterns, in ancient shrines and temples, and were later developed for use in tea gardens. They have been used since ancient times for visitors to rinse their mouths and wash their hands in an act of purification prior to entering the shrine or temple. Usually made of cut stone 600 to 900mm (2' to 3') high, at a convenient height for washing, this type of basin was called a *chozubachi* and is still used in gardens, adjacent to the verandah. When basins were introduced into tea gardens, they were developed into the *tsukubai,* meaning 'crouching bowl'. These are lower in height than the *chozubachi* to force guests to stoop while washing. This act of humility, in addition to the act of purification, produced the cleansing of both mind and body considered necessary before

partaking of the tea ceremony. Some *tsukubai* basins are 500 to 600mm (1' 8" to 2') high, others at ground level.

In accordance with everything in the tea garden, the basin has to be both functional and aesthetic and in harmony with the atmosphere of *wabi* and *sabi,* as explained in Chapter 2. They are of varying shapes made from natural stone with a depression 100 to 300mm (4" to 12") deep, cut into the top to contain the water. Sometimes they are made from old stones such as millstones, foundation stones or the pedestals of old lanterns, which lend the history of the stone to the water basin. Often a geometric basin is deliberately chipped to give it more of a natural, worn look. Some are made from stones of an unusual shape, such as the *sodegata chozubachi,* or the

'sleeve-shaped basin', at Joju-in, or the *tsukubai* at Ryoanji.

In the West, water basins can be difficult to find. Real stone ones can be imported from the Far East, but reconstituted stone basins are available, albeit in a limited range of styles. Similar types of materials are used as for stone lanterns, and it is instructive to look at an old reconstituted stone basin to see how it weathers. Stone urns are more easily available and would be acceptable in spirit if not truly Japanese in form.

Water basins are either replenished by directing a stream through a bamboo pipe set over the basin — the pipe being connected to the house water supply with an intervening tap — or fed from a circulation pump set below the basin in a separate chamber. In the latter case, the water should not be drunk. Alternatively, the water can be refilled regularly by bucket. If a stream or house water supply is used, the overflow water should be led to a drain, or should in itself become the source of a stream. If a circulation pump is used, the overflow water will drain back into the pump chamber, as demonstrated in Chapter 5.

As far as positioning is concerned, it is good to partially conceal the water source, so a preferred location is just in front of evergreen shrubs or a bamboo fence, on a low, flat, wide area. It is best not to place the basin near waterfalls or wells, because that puts the water elements in competition with each other. A stone lantern placed nearby will give illumination and help balance the mass of the basin. Stone basins provide a linking element between house and garden and therefore are often placed by verandahs.

Another common position is any point along a path. If the basin is not to be used for purification, it can be a place to wash one's hands after garden maintenance and, finally, water is of course a wonderful play element for children. Traditionally, a wooden ladle is placed on the basin for the purpose of drawing water out.

The traditional setting for a water basin is on the edge of a 'sea' of water-worn cobbles in a shallow enclosure, which acts as a drain for overflow water or that falling from the process of washing. Surrounding the area are rocks which both create a balanced composition and assist the participants in washing. A low, flat rock is placed for standing on, to the left is a rock smaller in size than the basin, on which to set down things you are carrying, and to the right a similar rock on which to stand a pitcher of hot water in winter. All these functions may be irrelevant to your actual usage of the water basin, but by keeping to this pattern the essence of Japanese gardens can be captured and the whole composition will both look and feel right.

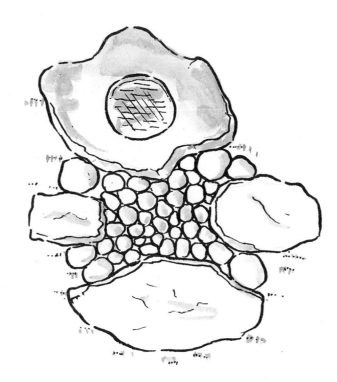

Traditionally, the arrangement of stones around a water basin consists of a low, flat rock in front for standing on, a smaller rock on the left to set things down upon and another on the right for a pitcher of hot water. Line drawings show how cobble infill provides drainage.

Shishi-Odoshi

The *shishi-odoshi*, or 'deer scarer', was originally used by farmers to scare off deer and boar to prevent them from damaging crops. It consists of a bamboo striker balanced between wooden supports on a pivot (see below). Water is fed from a bamboo pipe into the top of the bamboo striker. As the water collects, the striker falls forward under the weight of the water, the water spills out and the striker rises back up. When it does so, the striker hits a small rock, making a loud 'clacking' sound. The striker then begins to fill with water again and the cycle continues. *Shishi-odoshi* are sometimes used in gardens, as their movements provide an element of change and suggest the passage of time, but they are too intrusive to be used in a small garden. An added complication is that a water supply is needed and some adjacent higher ground from which to direct the water.

A shishi-odoshi, or deer scarer, is fed water from a bamboo pipe. When full, it swings down, discharges the water, and then swings back so that the end hits a rock and makes a loud clacking noise.

Stupas and Buddhas

A *stupa* is a stone tower which, by careful positioning, can affect the perspective of a view. By surrounding it with other scaled-down elements, a *stupa* will help to create an illusion of distance, at the same time providing a focal point. It should be placed at some distance from the viewer, partially screened by planting to give it added mystery. *Stupas* sit well by streams or ponds where the reflection in the water adds a further dimension, their upright shape contrasting well with the flatness of the water; or siting one part of the way up a planted mound or beneath trees can suggest a mountain temple. *Stupas* and Buddhas are used to bring a spiritual atmosphere into the garden. Buddhas need to be treated differently, as they should be seen close to. Position them near paths, with perhaps a hill or evergreen shrubs as a backdrop. A garden can accommodate one or two such pieces but they should not be over-used. Like many of these Japanese ornaments, both Buddhas and *stupas* are difficult to obtain in the West, but limited patterns are available in reconstituted stone.

An imposing stupa *at the Heian Shrine creates no illusion of distance; rather, it seems out of scale in this garden.*

Enclosures

The reasons for enclosure and the different types and situations were explained in Chapter 3. There are two main expressions of enclosure: one as boundaries with their associated gateways, and the other as screens for division within the garden. The basic materials used for these are wood, bamboo, mud, plaster or rendered wall.

Originally walls were of mud with a plaster finish, sometimes with timber framework, and a clay tile coping, as

A brushwood fence set in an unusual framework. The rope ties are functional as well as decorative.

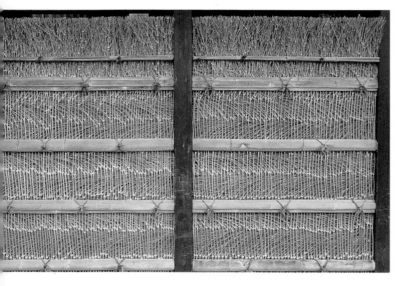

can be seen surrounding many of the old temples in Japan. Ryoan-ji is perhaps the best-known example where the wall also provides a neutral backdrop to the composition in front. Gardens using the principle of *shakkei* sometimes use a wall as an interface element between the garden and the distant view to be borrowed. The important point is that the wall should not compete with the composition in front of it, and therefore a plain textured finish is preferred. If you are starting anew, a rendered brick or block wall with a tile coping is the best choice. Incidentally, tile copings are as common in certain regions in the West as they are in Japan. The texture of a brick wall is really too distracting and, if already existing, is best rendered. The render should be painted in an off-white or yellow-brown colour range, or else use a white cement in the render. Remember, if you are using the *shakkei* principle, the wall height is dictated by the distant view.

Fences are used both for the boundary and for screens within the garden. Made of timber or bamboo, they were first used extensively in the twelfth and thirteenth centuries and the number of designs blossomed with the success of the tea gardens. As with most elements in a Japanese garden, they should be both practical and aesthetic. Bamboo fences give a garden a very Japanese ambience and the range of designs is extensive, tending to be named after the temples or gardens in which they were first constructed. There are two main types: those that are solid, and those that are perforated and can be seen through.

Daitoku-ji-gaki

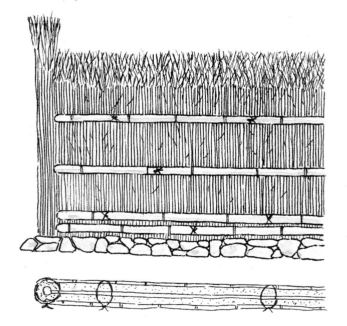

Koetsu-gaki

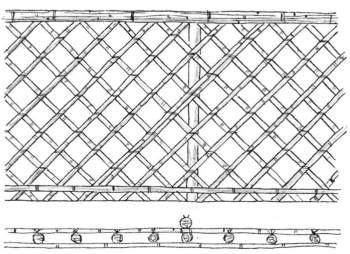

Bamboo fences are normally supported either by posts or by a timber frame to which are attached whole or split bamboo canes, in sizes and spacings that vary with the design. Nowadays, the canes tend to be nailed or wired unobtrusively, and then the twine ties added afterwards. The ties are an art in themselves. It is possible to make such fences in the West if supplies of bamboo are available, but you should be warned that such fences are usually short-lived.

Similar bamboo fences are often used for screens within the garden to control or direct views, to direct pedestrian movement, or to provide a backdrop to emphasize a particularly important element such as a water basin or lantern. Adjacent to a building, a *sode-gaki*, or 'sleeve-fence', is often used as a partial screen. It looks like the spread sleeve of a kimono and is made by entwining split bamboo or the branches of plants within a framework. These are definitely not for amateur construction and even in Japan are bought ready-made rather than being put together on site by garden workers.

Timber fences are made of solid timber boards or brushwood, both set in a timber framework. Brushwood fences are very rustic-looking and are stocked in the West by some fencing suppliers. They can be used as supplied or adapted to suit your design; or, indeed, you can construct a timber fence yourself using brushwood or trimmings fixed in a timber frame. The fence will last longer if some type of weathered coping is included.

Gateways are important and roofed gateways are particularly attractive. They not only celebrate the entrance but provide welcome shelter during rain. At the main entrance to a house they emphasize the division of public and private space, and within the garden they formalize the entrance from one part of the garden to another. Tea gardens employed gateways in this way to divide inner and outer garden. If roofed, then thatch, timber boards or shingles are used.

A bamboo fence at Katsura, looking rather weathered. Fences do need to be regularly replaced.

Teppo-gaki

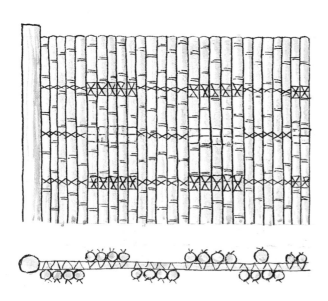

Yotsume-gaki

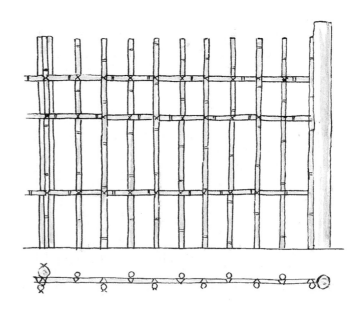

Planting

As with the arrangement of other elements, with planting the guiding principle is nature. Going out and taking a cursory look at plants in natural situations is not enough; you have to analyse the composition in terms of type of plant, pattern of growth, height and spread, density, preferred position and so on. Having analysed, you must then synthesize, simplifying and refining your acquired knowledge and selecting those plants which, if arranged in a certain way, will become symbolic of some part of nature.

Right: Planting in a Japanese garden is mostly evergreen, as demonstrated here at Ginkaku-ji. With pines a frequently used tree, the structure of the gardens is as evident in winter as it is in summer.

Below: A natural bamboo grove in its full glory. With the play of sunlight, the form of the stems and the tracery of the leaves, it is easy to see why the Japanese revere bamboo.

Preferences

As with any planting design, a decision on where to position plants must take into consideration certain basic characteristics of soil and the plant species being considered. Except for those used in a waterside location, all plants need good drainage so that their roots do not sit in water. If a site is poorly drained, either because of the nature of the subsoil or because it has been disturbed, then this must be improved before anything is planted. Alternatively, you can use species that will tolerate waterlogging, but your choice is then limited.

Plant species vary in their preference for soil acidity or alkalinity (known as pH), shade or sun, dryness or moisture and their exposure to cold. You may decide you want a particular species to go in a certain place in a composition, but it is no use planting it if the conditions are not suitable. This book does not attempt to describe the requirements of plant species in detail, and specialized reference books should be consulted. At the end of the book, however, there is a selected list of plants that can be used effectively in Japanese gardens in the West.

Enclosure

Chapter 3 described a number of functions for plants, one of which was the creation of enclosure. All compositions need a backdrop, and evergreen trees and shrubs can provide this in a homogenous green, in front of which other elements can be positioned. Typical plants used as a backdrop are small-leaved, non-variegated species with either insignificant or no flowers, which can easily appear to be in the distance. Unless *shakkei* is being used, hedge plants should be left to grow naturally; if their growth needs to be restricted, then they should be lightly pruned so that the hedge keeps its natural look. If earth mounds or hills are used for enclosure, planting evergreen shrubs and ground cover will normally give them an effective green cladding.

Planting is a favourite means of screening undesirable views, and very often the amateur gardener immediately thinks of evergreen conifers and the ubiquitous Leyland cypress, which is a very dull, short-lived species whose only useful attribute is that it grows fast. Instead of these, try a number of other evergreens such as *Thuja*, *Ligustrum*, *Chamaecyparis* or bamboo, which give a better effect and can be planted at a large size if a more immediate screen is desired. Deciduous plants can also provide screening, if you choose species with a dense branch structure so that in winter the undesirable views are at least obscured, if not totally blocked out.

Contrast

With the preponderance of evergreens, the contrast between them is not marked, but the Japanese relieve this by interposing a few deciduous or flowering plants to give an unexpected and therefore powerful contrast. The evergreen azalea is used for its massing quality, which lends cohesiveness to a design and in late spring unfolds to give a brilliant splash of colour. There are, of course, some contrasts between broad-leaved evergreen shrubs and needle conifers — for example, in their colour, form, leaf shape and texture. It is interesting to note the subtle variations in the green colours of different species.

The subtle contrasts among most plants are counterbalanced by the vivid differences between plants and other elements. The dark green leaf colour, soft consistency and open form of plants are the antithesis of rocks, gravel and stone ornaments. Once a bamboo fence has weathered to its light brown hue, plants really stand out against it.

The change in seasons can be appreciated only through the careful selection of plants. You can even chart the different months by the parade of effects and colours that appear from winter through to late spring — *Hamamelis* is followed by camellia, followed by apricot, cherry and then azalea. For their autumn leaf colours, plant the maples, *Ginkgo* and *Parthenocissus*. In winter, the characteristic bark effects of the birch and other deciduous plants provide a contrast to the evergreens. Except for the azalea and cherry these seasonal changes are not marked by a blaze of colour but simply by certain well-placed specimens, rather in the way that flowers are appreciated just through one selected piece placed in the *tokonoma* of a traditional Japanese house.

Opposite, top: *Blossom emphasizes the change in the seasons. For tea gardens, only the apricot is considered appropriate, but here at the Heian Shrine the more showy cherry provides a spectacular picture.*

Opposite, bottom: *Contrasts are important, and here the upright form of the iris is balanced by the horizontal form of the bridge. Additionally appealing are the dramatic but short-lived iris flowers.*

Selection

Planting is an important element of most compositions, even if it is somewhat subordinate to rocks. Having decided on a theme for a garden or landscape, the plants should be chosen to complement that theme. Thus, if there is to be a deep and mysterious waterfall, this atmosphere can be heightened by dark green plants on either side of the rocks. Marginal or waterside plants grow naturally beside streams, but in a Japanese garden, where water is often there to symbolize a mountain stream, it is common to have only a few plants along the bank, to emulate the natural scarcity of plants in that environment. If the water course is re-circulated, it is better that the plants are not actually in the water but on the edge, and therefore plants preferring moist rather than saturated soil should be chosen. If the stream is 'dry', composed only of gravel or pebbles, then the number of plants should be limited even more.

Ponds vary in their amount of planting. A marshy pond probably has the most, with reeds and rushes, or maybe just a huge bed of irises. An upland pond or water body, representing a seashore, does not have many marginal plants but instead has pines and evergreen shrubs behind the rocks that edge the pond; the pines are often trained out over the water. In certain compositions, water lilies and lotuses can be used in the water itself. If you decide that it should be a balanced ecological unit, then other floating and submerged aquatic plants will need to be introduced.

Josiah Conder's drawing of a tea garden showing different clumps of trees, bushes, plants and grasses arranged in an unkempt manner to create 'a wild and gloomy effect'.

To create a 'dewy path', emulating a tea garden, a very limited range of plant species should be used in order to reinforce the atmosphere of *wabi* or *sabi*. Only species that naturally grow wild on hills are usually planted. You should not, therefore, include flowering trees except the apricot, *Prunus mume*, as this has only modest blossom in the spring. Suitable shrubs are evergreens with glossy foliage, such as *Aucuba*, with ferns around the base of the rocks as typically occurs in nature. Both tall and dwarf species of bamboo are, of course, common and give an immediate cue to Westerners that the garden is in some way oriental.

Traditionally the floor of the 'dewy path' is moss-covered, but without the humid climate of Kyoto this can be difficult to achieve. In Japan, moss is commercially grown on a clay soil and is sold as moss turves, rather as grass turves are sold in the West. Although such an instant moss covering is not available in the West, it is possible to grow it by planting sprigs of moss on clay soil in the shade and providing irrigation in the form of a spray. The only problem with this is keeping the birds off. An easier, alternative means of achieving a kind of low ground-hugging texture, without the many problems encountered with moss, is to use other ground-cover plants.

Scale

Scale of plants is important in a composition. In Japan, root-balled or pot-grown shrubs and trees are usually planted when almost at the mature height and spread required for the design. Where possible this practice should be imitated, otherwise the composition will look unbalanced for the early years, the smaller plants being out of scale with rocks and ornaments. If large enough plants are not available, or are too expensive for the budget, then small ones should be used throughout, so that the garden has a consistent immaturity and looks like a garden in miniature. Ground covers are an exception, because once planted most spread quickly.

The scale of plants is influenced by the way they are grown. The Japanese like certain plants to have a weather-beaten look — as though they have been growing for decades on some exposed rocky promontory. Weather-beaten plants usually have a substantial trunk, from which branches have been broken off at different times by storms, so that the plant has regrown with an overall twisted appearance. Pines, and to some extent maples, are sought with this shape, and the Japanese achieve it by training the plant during its growth in the nursery. Finding good examples is difficult in the West, but the method of training is described in Chapter 5.

Perspective

The exaggeration of perspective often relies on planting to make it work. A feeling of distance can be achieved by placing plants with bright colours near the viewpoints, with those of darker shades further back. A similar effect is created if trees with large leaves are positioned in the foreground and those with smaller leaves, giving a finer texture, placed in the background. The use of large plants in the foreground and smaller ones in the background to give the illusion of distance, and the reverse to reduce distance, was discussed in Chapter 3. Try using a group of plants in the foreground or middle distance to screen certain background areas of the garden, making them only just visible. Tree trunks in the foreground create a frame for the view, which increases the sense of depth beyond.

The essential division or interface between garden composition and view in a *shakkei* landscape is often a hedge. In some historical gardens the hedge is a mixture of species and it is difficult to know if this was originally the case. When creating a new hedge, a single species will be most effective, as it does not distract from the garden composition or the view beyond. Shoden-ji employs *shakkei*, but instead of hedges it uses other interesting elements, such as clipped azaleas and camellias in groups of three, five and seven, which seem to represent rocks.

Many of the rules laid down for rock groupings apply equally to plants. The principle is asymmetry — grouping in threes, fives and sevens, and planting in triangles. The spacing of plants depends on their maturity at planting. For mature or semi-mature specimens the spacing is easy, because they will not spread out much more, but with smaller plants if you wish to get an instant effect you will have to plant them fairly close together and then thin them out as they grow

chapter 5

Design and Construction

The process of design and construction needs expertise and sensitivity to achieve something approaching authentic Japanese style. The first decision to make is who will design the garden or landscape space, and who will execute its construction. There are several options: if you feel you have the theoretical knowledge and an aptitude for the practical skills, you can do both the design and construction yourself; otherwise you can commission someone else to do it for you. If you decide on the latter you have the choice either of employing a designer for the initial design work and then using a landscape or garden contracting firm for actually carrying out the construction or, alternatively, there are many contractors who will offer a design and construction service, some of whom may be proficient in Japanese gardens.

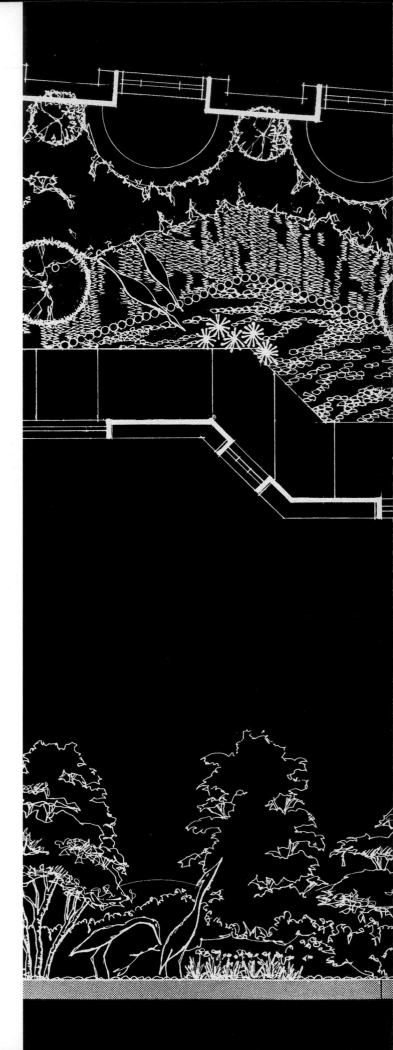

A plan and elevation forming part of the design process in the creation of a Japanese garden in a basement office courtyard behind the Strand in London. The concept in this dry garden is that water appears to flow from the waterfall on the right towards the left and under the building. (Designer: Philip Cave Associates)

Using a Designer

If you decide to employ a designer, first make sure they have a formal qualification and/or experience in the design of Japanese gardens. Most countries have some sort of institute or association of landscape architects or garden designers, which has laid down certain entry qualifications to its members. Britain has the Landscape Institute in London, and in the USA there is the American Society of Landscape Architects in Washington. By commissioning someone who is a member of a relevant and reputable institute to carry out your design work, you are assured that a certain standard has been attained.

The designer should be commissioned to produce a design showing the location of the various elements required, which can be approximately costed. Once you have approved it, working drawings and specifications can be produced which show how the design is to be constructed, what types and sizes of plants are to be used, and where they are to be planted. The designer can then obtain quotes from one or more landscape or garden contractors for carrying out the work. Each contractor will be submitting a price for the same scheme and therefore a direct comparison can be made.

References should then be taken up for the chosen contractor before appointment, and the designer should be asked to inspect the work as it proceeds to make sure it is executed correctly and to a high standard. You will probably find the designer's inspections on site will involve a lot of time selecting and approving materials, and positioning them in the scheme. Remember, in this option the designer works for you and will therefore have your interests at heart.

If, on the other hand, you decide on a design and construction package, choose your contractor carefully — the best way is by personal recommendation. Look at plans and photos of their previous projects and take up references. Make sure that they undertake a two-stage process, the first stage being the preparation of drawings and specifications, and the second stage being the construction work. They may be willing to do the design work 'on spec', but in the event of you not liking the design they may ask you for a design fee.

When you approve the design and specifications, study them carefully to make sure you are in agreement with the proposals and that everything has been covered. Each plant needs to be written down with the size at which it will be planted. For the larger shrubs and trees, measure out their sizes in the garden to check that they are what you had in mind. Remember that smaller plants cost less.

You should enter into some form of contract, even if it is merely an exchange of letters that refers to the plans, specifications, dates for commencing and completing the work, and the timing of payments. It is prudent to include some small retention of money that will be paid six or twelve months after completion, with the proviso that any defects coming to light during that period will be put right before the retention monies are paid. Defects would include such items as plants that die, paving that breaks up or sinks, mortar that breaks out, ponds that leak or pumps that do not function. It can be difficult to determine why a plant dies — it may be because of poor-quality stock, defects in the soil or planting technique, wrong position in the garden, lack of moisture or nutrients. As some of these reasons are related to maintenance, some contractors will only guarantee plants if they carry out the maintenance themselves. For a medium or large-scale project, therefore, it is preferable that the contractor carries out the necessary maintenance during the defects period (a minimum of twelve months is advisable for this).

The design and construction of a Japanese garden need a great deal of specialist expertise — first to design the space, then to choose the rocks and plants and to position them, together with the construction of water areas, paving and so on. This goes outside the scope normally encountered in Western garden design and construction, and it requires specialist knowledge and a genuine sensitivity to the art of Japanese garden design. It is quite easy to use all the necessary materials but to assemble them in such a way that the resulting garden is in no way Japanese in style, influence or even in spirit.

Briefing

Whether you decide to draw up your own design or get outside help, there are several fundamental questions to be considered; a commissioned landscape architect or garden designer will no doubt ask you them. First of all, what is the purpose of the garden or landscape space, and what activities does it need to support? It may be purely visual, to be viewed from the windows and verandah of the house, and walked in only for the purpose of maintenance. Alternatively, it may be for sitting, lying, contemplating, walking, entertaining in, or for children to play in.

It must be said that the traditional Japanese style lends itself to certain activities and not to others. What we think of as Japanese does not seem to fit in with such activities as children's play, hanging out washing or even entertaining. It is not that the Japanese do not perform such activities in their gardens but that they divide up the whole garden into areas to accommodate different functions. (An example is shown below.) The lounge may open out on to a Japanese-style garden, but this is probably divided from the area adjacent to the back door in which are located washing-lines, waste-bins and perhaps an area for growing vegetables. The approach to the front door could also be in a Japanese style but separated from the driveway. These separations and divisions can be achieved by a fence, wall or screen of hedge planting.

If you are using a landscape architect or garden designer, discuss with them at the outset everything that you seek from a garden including any favourite themes, natural scenery with which you have an empathy, and any other gardens that you particularly like. It may not be possible to accommodate all your desires, as some may conflict with others or the area may be just too small, but it is the job of the landscape architect or garden designer to assimilate your requirements and come up with a design that satisfies as many as possible.

Below, left: *Typical garden divisions around a Japanese house with the functional part separated from the formal garden by a fence or hedge.*

Below: A design for the roof garden of a private house in London, where the lower garden is Japanese in style and separated from the upper garden which is more Western. (Designer: Philip Cave Associates)

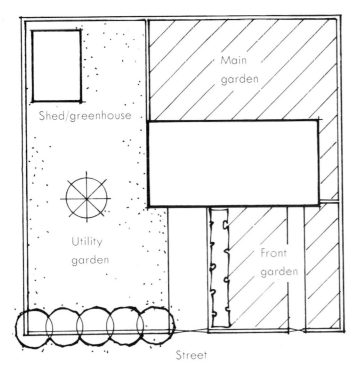

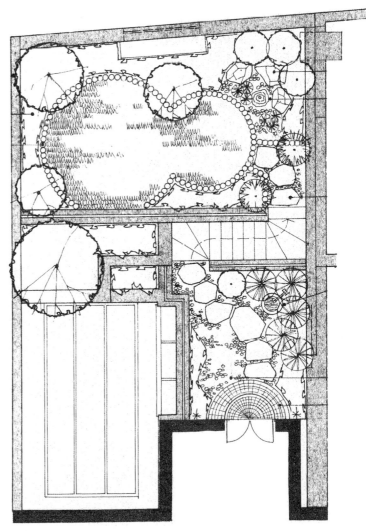

Survey

Before designing on paper can begin, a survey must be drawn up of what already exists in the garden or landscape space. For a small, detailed garden this should be drawn on a scale of 1 to 50, or 1 to 20 (i.e. 1 metre representing 50 metres, or 1 metre representing 20 metres); for a larger garden, in areas where detail is not proposed, a 1 to 100 scale will do.

If there is a building to be incorporated within the design it is best to start with this and measure out from it, as buildings usually have 90-degree angles that are easily drawn out. Every door and ground-floor window should be marked on the plan, including the height of the window sills above ground level, and the direction in which the door opens. The height of the sill is needed to ensure that any plants chosen will not block the window. Boundary fences and walls should be measured and marked on the plan, including their type of material, the position of any gates, and any existing paths to be retained.

The position of manhole covers and gullies should be shown, as drainage water from the garden may need to be connected to them; in any case, the manhole covers need to be incorporated into the design. The position of all existing vegetation also needs to be plotted, except that which you have decided not to keep. Make sure you indicate all the trees, both those on your own site and those on neighbouring properties. The position and diameter of the trunk, and the height and spread of the branches, are all needed.

It is important that any changes in level are measured and marked on the survey. In a small garden it is usually adequate to mark out levels relative to the threshold of the house. This can be done simply using a straight timber board with a spirit level on top, and measuring the drop or rise in level as you go away from the house. In a large landscape garden with a lot of level changes, a proper levels survey using a theodolite will need to be undertaken. Existing levels at the base of trees need to be plotted as these should not be altered in the design.

The survey drawing should be drawn out on plain or graph paper, showing the scale and the direction of north — for aspect is most important in the design. Make a note of whether the different views from each side of the garden are open or closed in, and whether they are pleasant views to be retained or undesirable views to be screened.

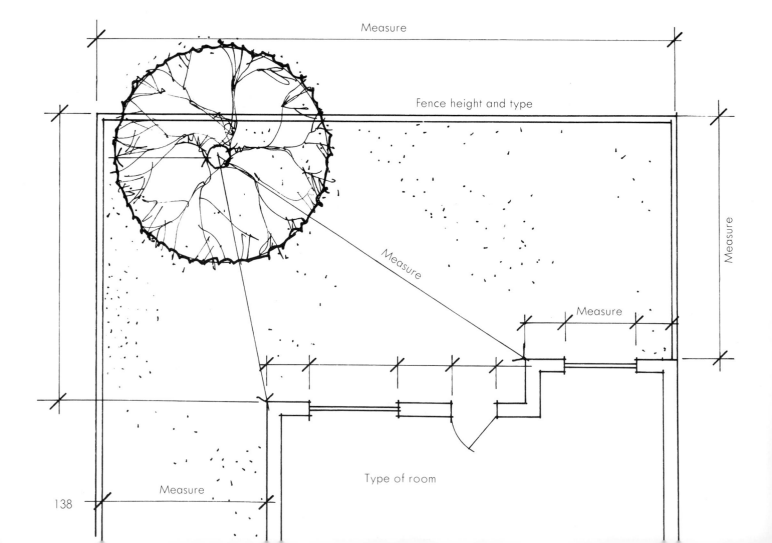

Ideas and Themes

Having decided to have a Japanese-style garden, you must then decide on a theme for the composition. Let yourself be guided by your emotions and your intuition in the first instance, rather than by practical considerations. You will be particularly drawn to some themes, not necessarily for any concrete reason, and you should follow that inspiration as far as possible. By responding in this way, the composition you create should have a meaning and significance that goes beyond the material senses, and the garden will affect you on all levels of your psyche.

You may, for example, feel a particular empathy for water in the form of rushing streams, smooth-surfaced ponds or the sea. Alternately, you may feel a oneness with rugged mountains, wooded slopes or moorland. Certain rock types or shapes, or plants growing in an unusual way, may trigger memories within you of particularly interesting scenery. If this scenery uplifted you in the past, introducing the essence of it in your garden can re-create that feeling.

Earlier chapters discussed the religious significance of certain islands, groups or rocks, or areas of gravel. There are Mount Sumeru, the mystical isles, and the *Sanzen* Buddhist triad, which will have a deep effect on you if such important concepts are part of your make-up — what Jung would call your unconscious mind. If they do have an effect on you in an unconscious way, then you should try to include them in your composition. If for you, however, they are just pieces of rock or mounds of earth, then it is better to choose that which does have some personal significance. The answer is always to look around your locality, your own country, and other countries that have inspired and influenced you, and to use them in your composition.

As well as these psychological influences, more practical reasons will help in deciding on the theme of the composition. An obvious factor is the size of space available — it is impossible to create a stroll garden in a courtyard, even with the technique of miniaturization! Some spaces are just too small to contain a pond garden with a waterfall and associated mound; for this a garden needs to have reasonable depth as well as width, so that the pond can recede into the background. Small spaces can, however, easily accommodate a *karesansui* or 'dry garden', or indeed a composition based on a tea garden.

The complexity of the composition in terms of construction can also be a deciding factor. If you are an experienced amateur and plan to undertake the construction yourself, bear in mind that 'real' water is more complicated to construct than 'dry' water.

Existing features — vegetation, levels, access — need to be taken into consideration. Rather than try and level a sloping site, incorporate it into the design. The presence of trees will restrict your movement of earth, as the level around them (normally as far as the branches spread) will need to be maintained. Limited site access, where all materials have to be taken through a house, or even in a lift up to a roof garden, may determine what can be accomplished. In this case, large rocks would be inappropriate, as would large trees.

A sketch of the dry waterfall arrangements and stepping-stone path layout for a new garden in the traditional style in Kyoto. (Designer: Kinsaku Nakane)

Design

The design stage is where creativity comes into play, and there are many reasons why design drawings are necessary. A plan shows where the various elements will be placed and draws out their approximate size. This enables you to be sure that the composition you have decided on is practical for the site, and you can begin to see how one element relates to another. It also enables you to calculate the materials necessary for the project by counting and scaling-off from the drawing. The design needs to be marked up on the survey drawing so that the existing features are always taken into account. You can either get several copies of the survey drawing done or else overlay it with some tracing paper.

The divisions in the garden should be drawn in and any

gates indicated to allow access at the right place. This is important for aesthetic reasons — to ensure that the composition is experienced in the way the design intended — and for practical reasons — so that the garden can be maintained easily, there is access to the garden shed, and the car can be taken out of the garage. Such divisions will be either fences or hedges, giving full or partial enclosure as the design demands. If the plot is new, the boundary enclosure can be decided on, again to fit the design.

Always keep in mind the aspect of the garden space (that is, which direction it faces). A space facing towards the sun is ideal; thus the backdrop, which is usually built up and shaded, is lit by diffused sunlight. This is important for waterfalls, to create a sense of depth and mystery.

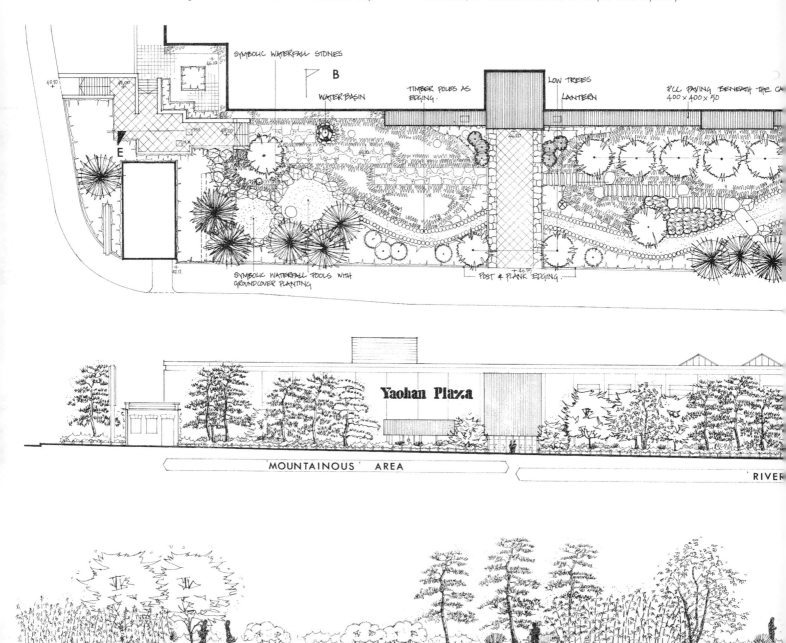

However, most aspects can be accommodated by angling the composition; in fact, a Japanese garden can easily be made in quite a tight, shaded space.

If ponds or streams are part of the composition, include them in the drawing, taking into account the desired position of paths, existing vegetation, hills, levels and viewpoints. Rock positions should be shown as rock groups, waterfalls or as edging to ponds and streams, and mark too the position of any ornaments. Finally, draw on areas for planting, either as specimens or as groups for massing.

As this design process proceeds, it is useful to draw elevations, sections or quick sketches of important parts of the composition so that you can appreciate the three-dimensional effect, as well as the form of it on the plan.

Design drawings showing the plan and elevations of a 200-metre-long Japanese garden in North London. It is a dry garden with winding water course commencing in the 'mountains' and finally discharging into the 'sea'. The middle elevation is the view from the main road and the lower one the view from the path that meanders through the garden. (Designer: Philip Cave Associates)

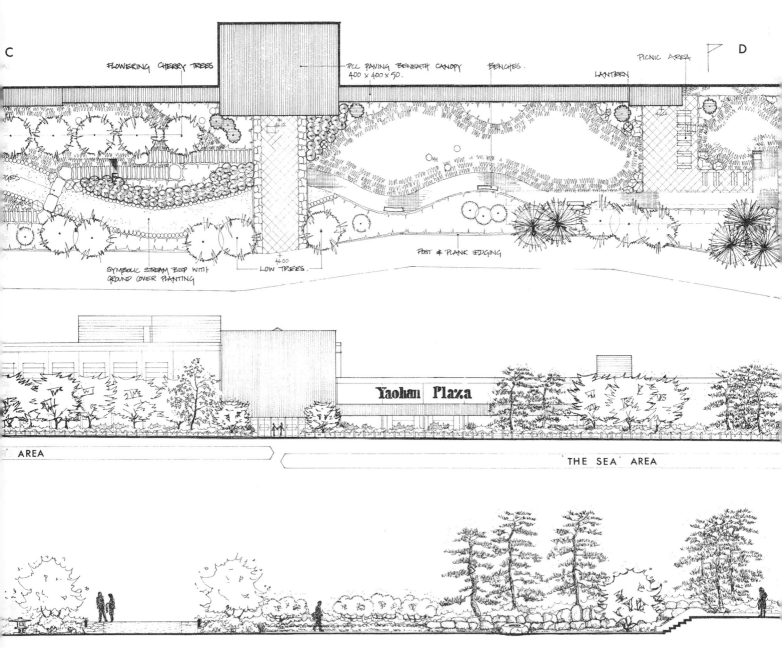

Creating Enclosure

The traditional mud and plaster wall described in Chapter 4 can be re-created using blocks or brickwork. To avoid frost problems, the wall should be built on a concrete foundation laid below ground on firm subsoil; a depth of 450mm (1' 6") is normally sufficient but is dependent on locality. Walls up to 1.8m (6') high can be a single brick (215mm/9") wide, taller walls will need to be at least one-and-a-half bricks wide (329mm/13½"), or even reinforced. The bricks should be bonded (as shown below) to give the wall strength.

To render the wall use a cement and sand mix to give a smooth finish. The render should be sealed before painting with an external paint finish. All walls need a coping as protection from the weather, and the Japanese favour a tile coping set at an angle to shed water. An existing wall can be modified, by rendering and renewing the coping.

To build a bamboo fence requires a good supply of either whole or split bamboo canes, according to the type of fence required, and twine for tying, which should be rot-proof and is best dyed black. A *yotsumegaki* is a low lattice fence (see p.125) which gives partial enclosure and, like most fences, is supported by timber posts. These posts should be treated timber set 450mm (1' 6") into the ground,

Below: Takegaki *fencing during construction, showing the split bamboo being slatted down. Right: Wall construction.*

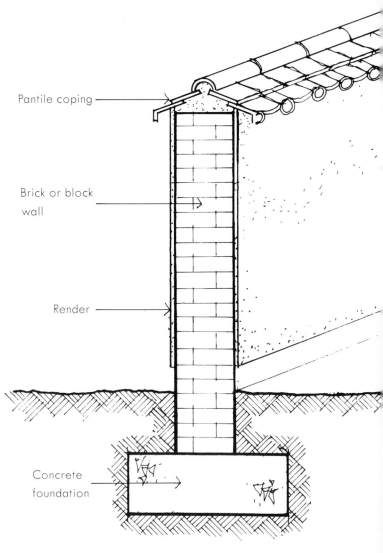

Pantile coping

Brick or block wall

Render

Concrete foundation

with 900mm (3') above the ground, secured by ramming hardcore around them at the bottom. The horizontal and vertical poles are whole canes, 30 to 40mm (1" to 1½") in diameter. Cut the horizontal pole to size, using a fine-toothed saw so as not to split the bamboo. Saw off the ends at a 45-degree angle, drill a hole through, and nail the pole to the wooden post with galvanized nails. Then cut the vertical poles to size and attach them to the horizontal poles using the twine. The vertical poles alternate front to back each side of the horizontal poles.

The construction of a *takegaki* fence is shown on p.142 (left). A softwood frame is built using sawn timber nailed or screwed together. The appearance of the frame is not important as it is completely covered by the bamboo. Split bamboo canes are then slotted down between guide strips and the softwood frame to lie horizontally above each other, the lower one sitting on a base of, say, granite setts (small paving blocks). At the top, a half bamboo cane is used as a capping and then more half bamboo canes, shaped at the top, are fitted vertically to the outside with galvanized nails or by tying them with wire. These are then finished off with twine ties.

A 'Moon-Entering' screen fence (left), so-called because of the aperture in the shape of a three-quarter moon, and a Korean screen fence in lattice work.

Creating Hills

In order to create hills or mounds, fill is required. It is best to use what fill material is available on site from the excavation of ponds or paths, otherwise fill will have to be imported from elsewhere. If you have a choice, it is wise to choose a free-draining subsoil material to avoid any drainage problems later. Before any earth-moving takes place, the area where the mound is to be created should be stripped of topsoil, as this will be needed to go back on the surface of the mound. Build up the mound by placing the subsoil in layers and lightly consolidating each layer before placing the next, as this will stop the mound from moving and eroding away. For shrubs and ground-cover planting, the mound should then be covered with about a 400mm (1' 4") depth of topsoil.

The height of the mound will be dictated by the size of the garden and the type of composition proposed. If, for instance, there is to be a waterfall at the rear of the composition which falls 1.2m (4'), then the mound will need to be built up to at least this height to make it look totally realistic.

Water Circulation System

Water must always remain clear and clean for it to keep its attraction. To achieve this it should either be kept moving and filtered, or be designed and maintained as a balanced ecological unit with the necessary range of marginal and aquatic plants, snails and fish to keep it healthy.

Unless one has a natural stream running through the property, a pump will be needed to keep the water moving and to re-cycle the water from the lowest point of the water course to the highest point. When choosing a pump there are a number of factors to be considered. First, there is the capacity you require, measured in litres per minute or gallons per hour. Second, there is the pressure necessary, measured in metres or feet of 'head' — which is the sum of suction lift, discharge elevation and friction loss through the pipes. The discharge elevation is the height of the outlet (or start of the water course) above the pump. As the head increases, so the output of the pump decreases.

Two types of pump are available: submersible pumps and dry pumps. Submersible pumps can be placed at the bottom of the pond or in a separate water chamber. Pipework is limited to an outlet pipe, which must be fed back to the start of the water course. The only other connection is the electrical cable to the pump. Dry pumps are located in a separate dry chamber, or pump house, with pipework leading to both the top and bottom of the water course.

Submersible pumps are generally preferable unless very large volumes of water are to be moved. Installation is easier because of the small amount of pipework, but the pump must always be submerged when in operation otherwise it will be damaged. Any noise from the pump is masked by it being below the water. The pump will have strainers to prevent debris from entering it, but if you wish to keep fish a filtration system is advised.

Various other mechanical devices can be included for water features. A drain in the bottom leading away to a good soakaway or surface-water drainage system is advisable for all but very small ponds. Overflow drains should be used if a rise in water level during periods of heavy rain would be critical, and must be included if the feature is fed by a natural stream. If the overflow is located at the side of a pond, debris will tend to collect there and can be easily removed. At its simplest, an overflow can be

Right: An overflow drain helps to avoid flooding caused by heavy rain. A simple mesh filter should be set in the neck of the overflow pipe to catch debris.

an outlet in the side of a pond protected by mesh and directed into a sump (see below). Any debris that gets through the mesh falls into the sump and can be removed. Excess water is then piped away to a drain.

Water-level sensors, which top up the water if it falls below a certain level, are another useful option. They are necessary if the water feature is not inspected regularly, as large fluctuations in level will affect a submersible pump, fish and plants. The simplest water-level sensor is a ball-valve chamber located on the edge of the pond and fed by mains water. The ball-valve is similar to those used in a domestic lavatory cistern and allows fresh water to flow in when the water level falls below a certain point. For a water feature inspected regularly, topping up the level by hose-pipe is adequate.

Pond Construction

The position and shape of ponds was discussed in Chapter 4, and now the method of construction and waterproofing needs to be covered. Any pond construction requires excavation, but the fill produced by this can often be used elsewhere in the garden for hills or mounds, especially if there is to be a tall waterfall. For any reasonable-sized pond you should consider using a mechanical excavator, hired with or without operator. The size of the project will determine the type of machine required. Before positioning a pond, do make sure that no drainage runs through the area, as this may be difficult to re-direct. If the pond is to have islands that are more than just rocks, it is best to leave the soil undisturbed for maximum stability. There is nothing more heartbreaking than seeing your island gradually sink down below water level.

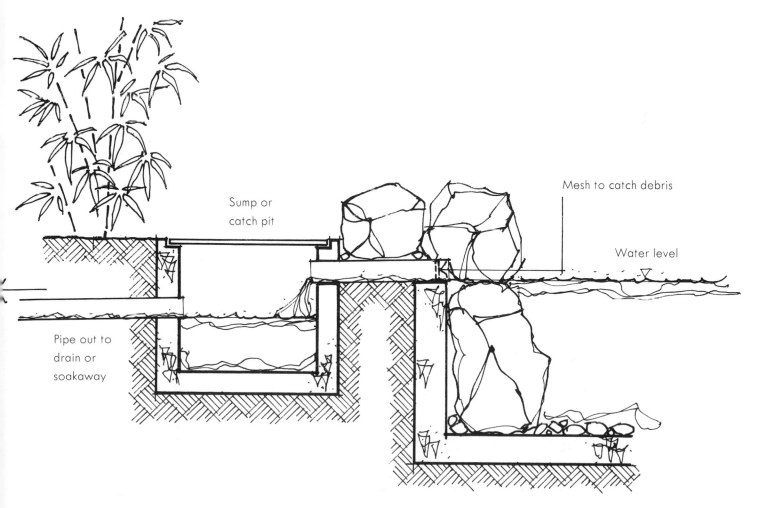

Sump or catch pit

Mesh to catch debris

Water level

Pipe out to drain or soakaway

Waterproofing

For waterproofing the age-old system of puddled clay can be used if the lake or pond is fed by a natural stream. The clay is placed in a layer at least 150mm (6") thick, and only certain types of clay are suitable. A clay system does allow you to use any type of edge treatment. If the pond is not fed by a natural stream, artificial materials can be utilized, but none of these should be visible once the pond has been fully completed. The most likely place where they will show is at the edges, and considerable attention needs to be paid to this area.

There are three main types of artificial material suitable for waterproofing: waterproof concrete, butyl lining and fibreglass. Waterproof concrete is a very strong and durable material, relatively easy to lay for a small pond in any kind of shape. All types of edges can be achieved, from vertical sides to shallow beaches, and such devices as drains are easily set in. When using concrete all the vegetable topsoil needs to be removed down to firm subsoil, allowing, of course, for the thickness of the concrete. Lay the hardcore about 100mm (4") thick and consolidate it. The thickness of the concrete and the possible need for reinforcement depends on the size of pool being created. A small pond can be successfully constructed using a 150mm (6") thickness of concrete with mesh reinforcement running through. Simple timber shuttering, to temporarily hold the concrete until it hardens, is necessary to construct the vertical sides, which should extend to just above the water level.

Larger ponds are more complex to build, requiring construction joints and sometimes expansion joints that have to be waterproofed, or steel reinforcement bars set in the concrete for strength. Sometimes an inner skin of asphalt tanking is applied, but all this could be problematic for the amateur.

Butyl liners are good for ponds of an informal shape. It is a very effective, clean material to use, but the edges need to be well-concealed, and it can be punctuated by sharp objects, so take care that nothing remains after excavating which could damage the lining. It is possible to create vertical sides with a butyl liner, but shallow beaches are more easily achieved. If the pond is larger than the largest size of liner sheet, then they will need to be joined. Instead of hardcore, lay 75mm (3") of sand and place the liner on top. As with concrete, the liner needs to extend above the water level by not less than 100mm (4"), or more depending on the size of pond.

At a beach edge, the liner is cut to size, allowing a minimum of a 300mm (1') flap to turn back (see below). Gravel, pebbles or rocks can be placed on the edge to disguise it and create a natural effect. A vertical-sided edge is achieved by taking the liner up and over a brick or concrete wall and lapping it under the coping. A drain can be incorporated in a liner but the fitting is a specialized one. There can be a problem with a butyl liner in a large pond, as gases such as methane may be produced and collect in gas pockets under the pond, then float up to the

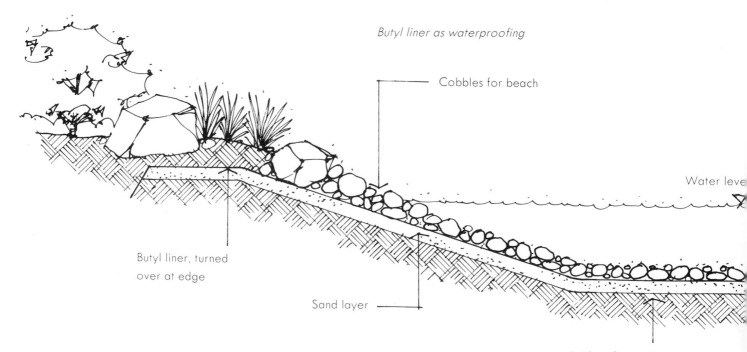

Butyl liner as waterproofing

Cobbles for beach

Water leve

Butyl liner, turned over at edge

Sand layer

Laid on firm soil

surface. This can be avoided by venting the layer under the liner with pipes.

Fibreglass, carried out *in situ* (on site), is a good medium for waterproofing. It is strong and can be moulded to any shape of pond and any type of edge. The only disadvantages are that it can be chipped if hard objects are dropped on it, and its application is really a professional operation. For a fibreglass lining, a thin layer of concrete should be set in the excavated area for the fibreglass to be moulded around. The fibreglass consists of a glass mat combined with wet resins in successive layers, with a finish or gel coat consisting of coloured plastics to give a smooth coloured appearance. Drains and other fittings can easily be incorporated in the operation. This type of fibreglass pond should not be confused with small pools that can be bought off the peg in some garden centres or from aquatic suppliers and which always seem to be produced in a garish blue colour.

The colour of the pond is important. Black is preferred, as it recedes into the background when seen between rocks and gives the water a reflective quality. Blues and greens, beloved by pool suppliers, should be avoided. Butyl is normally supplied in black, and black pigment can be used in the gel coat of fibreglass. Concrete needs to be coated to make it black, there being various types of waterproof paint available. All need recoating after a time.

A newly built concrete pond should be filled and emptied of water several times to flush out the lime content in the concrete, which is harmful to both fish and plants. In fact, it is advisable to leave the pond for several months before stocking it. Butyl-lined and fibreglass ponds are less of a problem but should also be flushed through and left to stand before stocking. Before fish are put into a pond the water should be tested for anything toxic. The pH, or degree of acidity or alkalinity, should be checked regularly and corrected if not near to neutral.

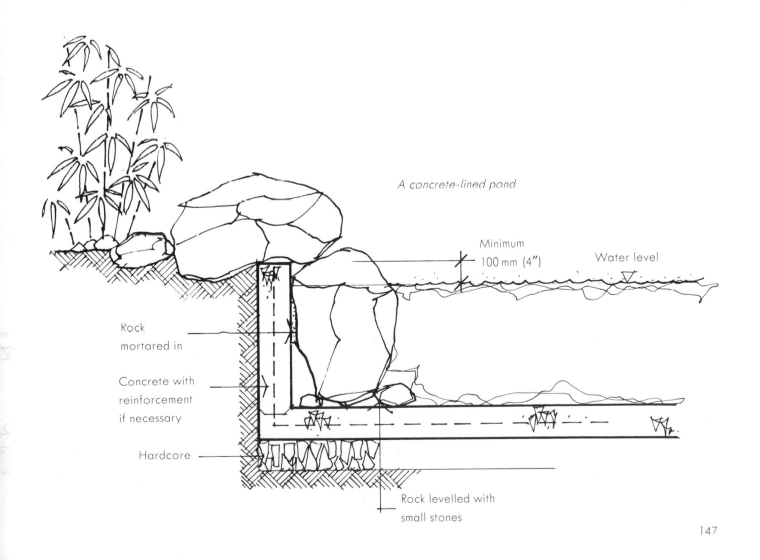

A concrete-lined pond

Minimum 100 mm (4")   Water level

Rock mortared in

Concrete with reinforcement if necessary

Hardcore

Rock levelled with small stones

Edge Treatment

Once the basic pond is finished, the edges need to be dealt with. If they are well designed the pond will look totally natural, but if the waterproofer is visible or the rocks are poorly set, then the pond will look unconvincing. The timber stakes mentioned in Chapter 4 are best used with the clay waterproofing, as they tend to puncture the other waterproofers, unless detailed cleverly. It is possible, however, to attach the stakes to vertical concrete sides.

Rock edges need slightly different treatments according to the method of waterproofing used. Generally speaking, it is more effective if the rock disappears well below the water level. With concrete pools, the rock is best set in mortar against the vertical side, with the top just protruding above the top of the concrete. Then earth or further rocks can be placed over the top of the concrete to conceal it. In fibreglass ponds, the rocks can also be set on a mortar bed, but in butyl-lined ponds they are better carefully embedded in sand or rounded gravel.

These guidelines apply to islands as well as the edges of the pond. To create small islands in a pond, a ring of rocks is set in the middle, as for edging a pond, and the gaps are filled with smaller rocks and mortar. The space is filled with small rocks and hardcore, which is finally topped with a half metre (1' 8'') or so of topsoil.

Beaches are easy to create for all types of pond. Simply cover a shallow slope with a layer of loose water-worn cobbles or pebbles to a depth of 50 to 100mm (2'' to 4''), depending on the size of the material. The beach should extend on to dry land to make it realistic — as always, use beaches in nature as your model. A beach is a particularly good way of concealing the edges of a butyl liner. Small rocks laid on a slope can also provide an interesting edge, reminiscent of some rocky sea shores.

Bridges

Bridges need to be considered early on in pond construction. Single-span bridges need a firm foundation at each shore and the waterproofing has to accommodate this. Double-span bridges need a further foundation in the middle, and the base of the pond will need reinforcing to bear this extra weight, especially if the bridge is of stone.

Right: A waterfall in an interior garden in an office atrium.

Far right: The ribbed effect of this newly constructed waterfall will create a rushing sound.

Waterfalls

Having looked carefully at falls both in nature and in other gardens you are ready to construct one. It is advisable to sketch it out roughly in section and elevation, to work out where each rock will be placed and the size it might be. The points made later in the section on Rock Setting (see p.152) are applicable here.

The rocks will have been chosen in a stone company, nursery or garden centre and transported to the site. By the time of their delivery you should have a good idea where each one will go and which way up it will be. Watch the rocks being unloaded so that you can get to see any faces that were not visible when you selected them.

You will also by this time have decided on the type of waterfall — whether it is a single fall or a broken fall, the height of it, and the way it will face. The mound in which the waterfall rocks will be set should have been formed, probably by fill excavated from the pond.

The line drawing on p.149 shows the construction of a broken fall. First of all the lower rock is placed against a vertical face of the pond and mortared in. It is best if it comes up to the top of the pond lining so that the next 'water-falling stone' sits well on top of the pond lining. The shape of the top and lip of this stone is particularly important as it will determine how the water falls. These rocks should be angled so that water falls from their top down to the next rock. Then place the side stones, arranging them slightly in front to give visual stability to the group and to contain the water as it falls down. At the back

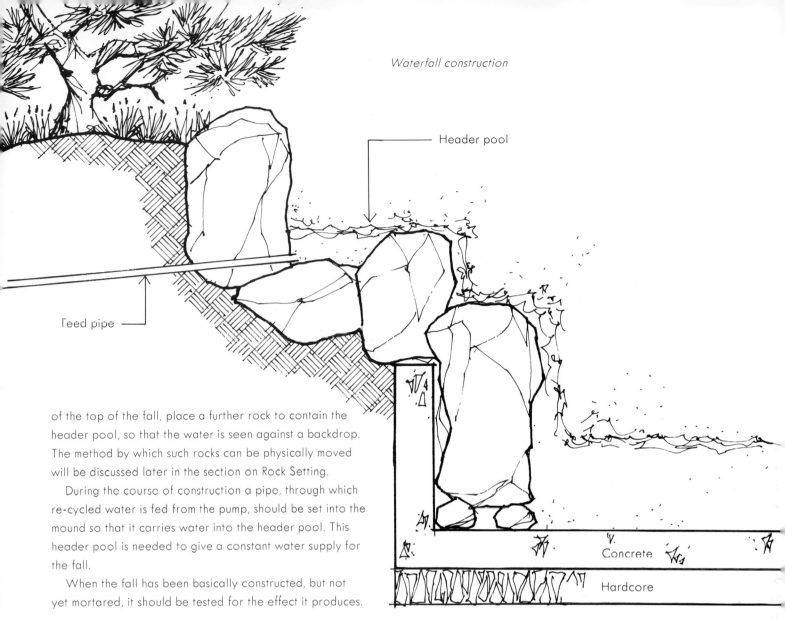

Header pool

Feed pipe

Concrete

Hardcore

of the top of the fall, place a further rock to contain the header pool, so that the water is seen against a backdrop. The method by which such rocks can be physically moved will be discussed later in the section on Rock Setting.

During the course of construction a pipe, through which re-cycled water is fed from the pump, should be set into the mound so that it carries water into the header pool. This header pool is needed to give a constant water supply for the fall.

When the fall has been basically constructed, but not yet mortared, it should be tested for the effect it produces.

Considerable adjustment is usually needed to get the weirs over which the water falls level, and the water falling as the designer intended. A lot depends on the amount of water being fed in at the top; for a reasonable effect there should be at least 10mm (just less than $\frac{1}{2}$") over the top weir.

Sometimes ribbing is added to create a rushing effect as the water cascades down (see left). Alternatively, the shape of the top of the weir may need to be adapted so that the water falls clear of the water-falling stone. With a large fall, a small pool can be introduced halfway down, which will then overflow, causing the water to complete the fall. Such a pool could be lined with butyl or created in concrete.

The possibilities are infinite. However, once the play of the water is to your liking, you should mortar the joints in the stones so that the water does not escape behind the fall. Plants can also be fitted into crevices in the rocks.

Streams

The course of a stream should be plotted on the ground according to the design drawing. On the slope of a stream, the *Sakuteiki* states:

> *... if you make the ratio of the drop in elevation to the distance of the running stream to be three to one hundred, the stream flows smoothly with a murmuring sound. However, towards the down stream where the garden landscape becomes gentle, the stream will flow being pushed by water from upstream, thereby without the need of dropping the elevation.*
>
> (Shigemaru Shimoyama)

Therefore, a slope of 3 per cent, or 1 in 33, should be considered a maximum, and can be decreased to be almost level and still achieve a flow. If the gradient of a stream is too steep, the water will just collect at the bottom. Thus, for a stream designed to traverse slopes steeper than this, a low weir should be introduced (see below). Such a weir should be formed by a flattish stone in the centre protected by larger stones at each side. The stream depth should generally be between 50 and 150mm (2'' and 6''), with gravel or cobbles placed at the bottom.

The points made earlier in this chapter on Water Circulation Systems, Pond Construction and Edge Treatments apply equally well to streams. A stream is best formed out of concrete or butyl liner. Any rocks used should be rounded and preferably water-worn, to look as though they had been in that particular stream for centuries, and they should be set low down. Rocks placed in the stream flow will increase turbulence and, temporarily, the speed and sound of the water. Lastly, and firstly, make sure accurate measurements are taken of levels in the garden, for water will not flow uphill.

A section through a concrete-lined stream

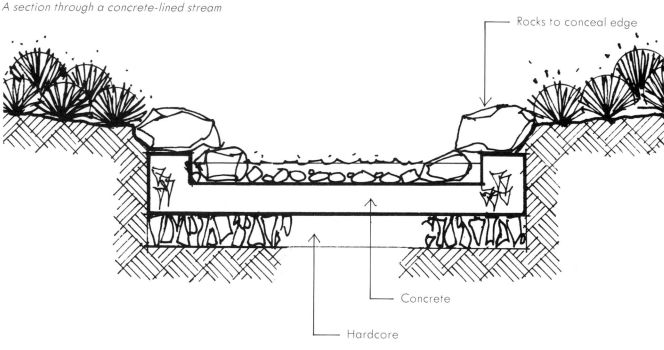

Rocks to conceal edge

Concrete

Hardcore

A long section with weir

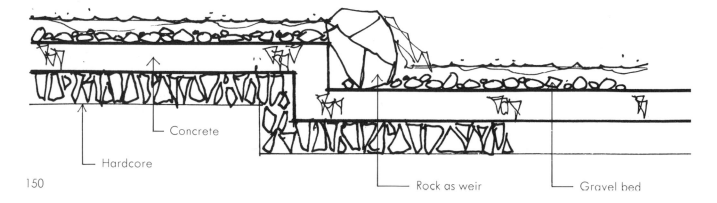

Concrete

Hardcore

Rock as weir

Gravel bed

'Dry' Water or Gravel Areas

Many of the instructions given for real water features apply to the *karesansui* or 'dry landscape', except of course that pumps and waterproofing are not needed. Edge treatments are the same, except that timber stakes can always be used as there is no waterproof liner to puncture.

The type of timber you use for these stakes will depend on what is available in the locality, but it should either be naturally resistant to rot or treated in some way. The only proper treatment for softwood is by vacuum pressure impregnation, for which the bark needs to be removed. The stakes should be cut to size before treating, as the preservative needs to penetrate the exposed end grain. Softwood can then be coloured using a decorative timber protection recommended for exterior use.

The line drawing below shows how the stakes are set into the ground. They need to be at least 400mm (1' 4") below ground level, but deeper if the height of soil retained is more than 600mm (2'). They are set close-butted in a trench with concrete or well-rammed hardcore around their base.

Dry waterfalls are constructed in a similar way to real waterfalls. They do tend to be simpler, using fewer rocks, but the sensitivity exercised in the choice of rock and its placement needs to be that much more refined. As explained in Chapter 3, the water-falling stone is particularly important in a dry garden. With broken falls, it can be effective to have a small pool halfway down, composed of gravel.

Dry streams are laid out as though water were to be present but no concrete or butyl base needs to be laid. Obviously, the gradient does not have to be precisely set out but it should not be too steep. If it is necessary for the stream to travel down a steep gradient, this should be achieved by stepping with weirs, just as you would do if water were present.

Both the bed of a stream and a larger body of water symbolizing a pond or sea are composed of gravel or cobbles. To create this the area needs to be excavated below the proposed, finished level of the gravel. The depth of gravel or cobbles needed varies with the size of their individual pieces, as the base needs to be completely covered. Crushed granite 5 to 15mm ($\frac{1}{4}$" to $\frac{3}{4}$") in diameter would need to be laid at a minimum depth of 75mm (3"), but deeper if it was to be raked into ripples or wave motions. Water-worn cobbles 25 to 50mm (1" to 2") in diameter need to be laid at a minimum depth of 100mm (4").

After excavation, the soil should be rolled level and a permeable filter membrane or fabric (such as Terram 500) should be laid out with the joints overlapped. The gravel or cobbles are then spread loose on top. The function of this filter membrane is to separate the gravel or cobbles from the soil below, while still allowing water to drain through. Perhaps more important, it deters weeds from growing. The filter membrane should be trimmed around the edges so that it is not visible.

Traditionally patterns are made in the gravel using a wooden rake with wide teeth. Modern metal rakes tend to have the teeth too close together, but it is easy to make up a wooden one using a timber board with notches.

Above: The gravel stream in this roof garden is edged by timber stakes which hold back the soil, as shown in the section below.

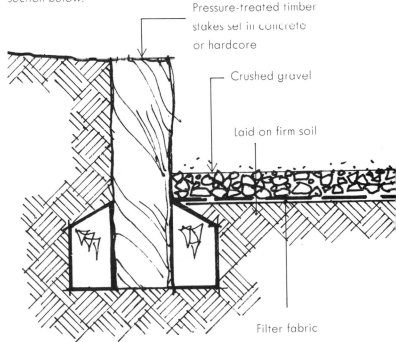

Pressure-treated timber stakes set in concrete or hardcore

Crushed gravel

Laid on firm soil

Filter fabric

Rock Setting

The initial design plan will show a certain number of rocks grouped in different ways and this must be the basis for choosing the rocks at the suppliers. From the plan, the rough size can be estimated, and from this an approximate tonnage calculated. This information plus any drawings and the knowledge that you have built up should aid in the selection of the rocks.

When choosing the rocks, as many faces as possible should be viewed to get a good idea which one should be considered the front and which the top. Most of these judgements are made by intuition, which only comes from looking at a lot of rocks and using them in projects.

When selecting large quantities, each rock should be marked in some way, preferably with road chalk or marking paint. I was somewhat annoyed, but later amused, when a stone company once offered me a marked rock saying that it was for another project but that they could easily find a substitute for the other customer. That other customer was me and the rock was for one of my other projects.

Once chosen, the rocks are transported to the site of the project. Make sure that the quote obtained includes transport, as this is a large proportion of the cost of the rocks. You should also stipulate that the rocks are off-loaded by crane or by hand, as tipping rocks off the end of a truck does them no good — you could end up with twice as many pieces as you intended!

Again, as with the rocks for waterfalls, watch them being unloaded, as you can often catch sight of a face that was hidden at the suppliers. They should be unloaded on to the ground or on to timber pallets in a storage area, each one individually placed at one level, with room to move around them. Stop anyone from piling them up, as that makes it impossible to select them in the order that they are required.

Moving the rocks around on site can be a problem. If a large number of rocks is involved, then a crane is essential as long as it can gain access to the site. In some instances, a crane with a long jib may be required to lift the rocks

Sketch of a dry waterfall composition for a private garden in Kyoto. (Designer: Kinsaku Nakane)

over a building. Ideally the rock should be lifted from the storage area to the final position in one operation, but this is rarely achievable. The more often they are moved, the greater the chance that they will be chipped or broken. For small numbers of rocks or tight spaces, rocks can be moved with a tripod, block and tackle or, as Japanese garden workers skilfully move them, slung by rope from a pole, which is then supported on their shoulders.

The first rock group to be positioned should be the one providing the main focus in a composition, and the first rock within that group to be set should be the central one. This may be a tall, vertical rock, as in the line drawing below (right), which shows a three-rock group. It is usually helpful to make a sketch of how the group should be arranged, even if this is modified as the setting proceeds.

Rocks should be set by at least one-third of their height into the ground to give them stability, both physical and visual (see p.96). Therefore, a hole should be dug about one-third of the height of the rock and the rock lowered into it so that the chosen top and front faces are exhibited. The rock needs to be looked at from the viewpoints to check that it is set correctly. At this stage one is not seeking overall balance, because other rocks will be placed around it, but you are looking for it to be at the desired height, with a stable feel to it in relation to the surrounding finished soil level.

If you decide that it needs to be raised or lowered, then it will need to come out of the hole, the soil level re-set and the rock put back. This is an easier operation to direct than to perform. When you are satisfied with the set of the rock, then earth or hardcore should be rammed around the base until it is firm. Only very tall rocks are likely to need concrete around the base to achieve stability, although when installed in a public place more caution is needed.

The next step is to set the second most important rock in the group, which is probably the next one down in size. Follow the same procedure as for the first rock. The concept of triangles already explained in Chapter 4 should be adhered to, with the rock positioned at one apex. This second rock needs to be set at the correct angle in relation to the surrounding soil, but it must also relate to the tall vertical rock, reinforcing its visual stability. The shape of the tops of rocks in a group is an important factor in creating a balanced composition, and any distinct strata or veining should be taken into account. Again, study the rock arrangement from the viewpoints.

Finally, a low flat rock is used to lead the eye in, to complete the composition and to give overall balance to the group. Bear in mind that the low flat rock may be three-quarters buried with only the top quarter showing. A three-rock group such as this can be enlarged into a five-rock or seven-rock group by continuing the process, or one rock of the group can be missed out and imagined, or its place taken by a plant. If it seems difficult to place a particular rock, try turning it over several times and new possibilities will reveal themselves. Once the group has been set, there are still opportunities to conceal an unfortunate junction with the ground by the use of a plant cleverly placed.

Stages of setting a rock group

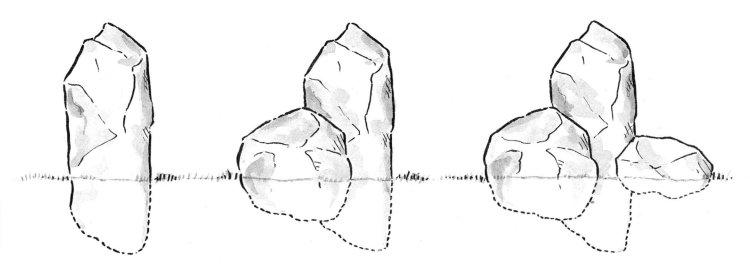

Bridges

The necessity to provide a good foundation for a bridge is particularly critical for stone bridges, with both the weight of the stone to support and the weight of any users. For all the single-span bridges described in Chapter 4, except for the *yatsuhashi* plank bridge and the stepping-stone bridge, the weight is borne by the foundation stones at each end. For a double-span bridge, an additional foundation stone is required in the middle. Foundation stones should have a flat face placed uppermost and be substantial pieces of stone. They should be bedded in firm subsoil or a layer of hardcore.

Bridge-supporting stones, placed at the four corners of the bridge, should be set well down in the ground so as not to intrude on the composition yet be substantial enough to balance the bulk of the bridge. The practical function of these supporting stones, which is perhaps more important with timber bridges than with stone, is to prevent the bridge from moving sideways.

Log and turf bridges are an interesting alternative to stone. The log bridge is made from timber support rails (either horizontal or arched), with logs 50 to 100mm (2" to 4") in diameter nailed or bolted tightly together on top. The logs should be treated and coloured as for timber stakes (see Edging Treatments), and the supporting timber

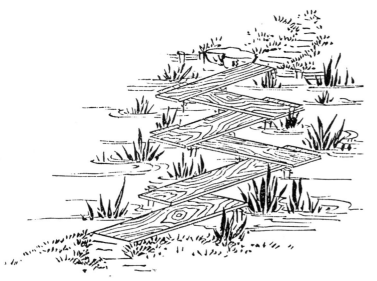

as for decking (see p.158). The nails or bolts should be galvanized.

The turf bridge is built in a similar way, except that planks are used instead of logs. The planks are overlaid by a clay subsoil and grass turves placed on top. It is beneficial if some heavy-gauge polythene, carefully concealed, is placed between the planks and the clay subsoil to help conserve moisture, as turf bridges can easily dry out.

The *yatsuhashi* plank bridge is easily constructed using timber support posts and planks. When it was introduced into gardens in the late Edo period, eight sets of planks were used. As shown (right), the planks can be supported on vertical posts, with a 100 × 100mm (4″ × 4″) cross-section, to which is bolted a supporting joist of 75 × 100mm (3″ × 4″). Timber planks, 50 × 200mm (2″ × 8″), are then laid on to the joists in pairs and screwed down. It is better to use two planks side by side, as wider ones tend to warp and collect water. The planks should be 150 to 200mm (6″ to 8″) above the water. If the pond is clay-lined, or it is a dry garden, the posts can just be driven down until firm, but if it is concrete-lined, the posts will have to be set in concrete. You need to make sure that the preservative used in the timber will not affect fish or plants. The sizing of the timber and the spacing of the joists depends on the expected load and the overall size of the structure.

Left: Characteristic Josiah Conder drawings of a yatsuhashi *plank bridge, and turf and stone bridges (left) and a wooden bracket bridge (below).*

Above: Detail of yatsuhashi *bridge, showing the vertical posts and supporting joists.*

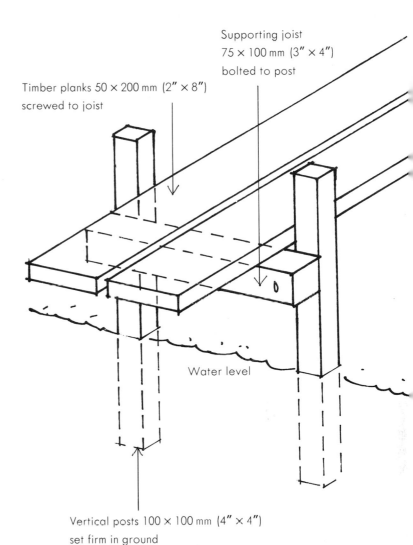

Supporting joist 75 × 100 mm (3″ × 4″) bolted to post

Timber planks 50 × 200 mm (2″ × 8″) screwed to joist

Water level

Vertical posts 100 × 100 mm (4″ × 4″) set firm in ground

Paths

In Chapter 4 the different types of stepping-stone paths and the shape of stones required for them were described. When you are ready to lay the path, set out the stones according to the design plan, choosing the ones which fit best against each other, and aiming to have relatively straight sides facing one another. Excavate a hole larger than the stone to be laid out but not quite as deep — when the stone sits in the hole, the flat top should be protruding just above the surrounding ground level. Soil should then be well rammed in around the stone until it is firm. Large, flat stones are best seated on some well-rammed hardcore, perhaps with a few dabs of mortar on the underside.

Stone pavements are composed of many stones of different shapes and thicknesses. The pavement with parallel edges is achieved by positioning stones with one straight side on the edge and infilling with other more irregular stones or cobbles. First excavate out the vegetable topsoil down to firm subsoil. Then, as with stepping stones, all the

materials should be laid out before you begin construction to see how the stones fit together. Old, weathered materials are always to be preferred.

Assuming only pedestrian traffic is proposed, a bed of well-consolidated hardcore 75mm (3'') deep is sufficient, making up with more hardcore if the excavation was too deep. Then a small aggregate concrete bed 50mm (2'') deep is laid, the stones are placed on top and tapped down to a uniform surface. A slight crossfall will ensure that water is shed to the side. The joints can be mortared up, but to just below the top level of the stones so as not to compete visually.

Gravel is a cheap natural paving material but it needs regular maintenance to look its best. This involves watering, rolling and weeding, plus topping up with more gravel as necessary. It is best edged with timber boards, natural rock or setts to prevent it from spreading. To make a gravel path the soil should be excavated, a bed of well-consolidated

hardcore or hoggin (mixture of sand and gravel) 75mm (3'')
deep laid, and then a layer of unwashed gravel or shingle
40mm (1½'') deep. Roll and water repeatedly. Unwashed
gravel is used because it contains clay particles that bind
the gravel stones together. Gravel or shingle varies with
the locality, so you should shop around to get the desired
effect.

Other materials that can be used are bark and log rings.
After excavation, wood bark can be used in a layer about
75mm (3'') deep. It should be approximately 10 to 30mm
(⅓'' to 1½'')-grade bark, which is a pleasing dark brown
colour, and should not contain woodchips, which are light-
coloured. Pine bark has a particularly nice smell. Log rings,
cut from hardwood, should be at least 150mm (6'') in
diameter. Embed them in firm subsoil with the bark left on.
The interstices can be filled with a light-coloured gravel or
pebbles for an interesting effect.

*Left: The rectilinear stone pavement at Katsura directs both
the eye and the feet and contrasts markedly with the
stepping-stone paths. The lantern on the left lights the way.*

*Below: The juxtaposition of the clean lines of the
rectangular stone pavement and the stepping-stone path
with its random infill makes a dramatic statement. The infill is
nicely softened by moss.*

Timber Verandahs or Decking

Decking can be used either adjacent to buildings or as freestanding platforms. Both are relevant to Japanese-style gardens: verandahs have been continually used for centuries in Japan, and platforms in the form of linking corridors were used in Shinden-style residences.

The type of timber available varies from place to place but softwoods are usually the most economical. They do, however, need to be treated to extend their life and the best treatment is vacuum-pressure impregnation, by which preservative is driven into the grain of the wood under pressure. Preservatives that are brush-applied tend to be short-lived as they get washed out. Pressure-impregnated timber can be supplied by most timber merchants. If timber is cut or drilled after being treated, the area of exposed wood should be treated with a brush-applied product.

Decks or verandahs at or near ground level on stable ground are easy to build, but you will need structural advice if they are free-standing and elevated more than 900mm (3'), or are on unstable ground. The line drawing opposite (top) shows a typical detail of a deck.

The supporting posts need to be connected to the concrete footing in some way. The detail opposite (top) shows a drift-pin, but other types of post anchors can be used. The posts should be 100 × 100mm (4" × 4"), or 150 × 150mm (6" × 6"). Two timber beams should then be bolted on each side of the posts. The joists sit on top of the beams. Typical dimensions for the beams and joists are 50 × 150mm (2" × 6"). The decking timber is then nailed down on to the joists. This can be 50 or 38mm × 100mm (2" or $1\frac{1}{2}$" × 4"), or 50 or 38mm × 150mm (2" or $1\frac{1}{2}$" × 6"). The planks of deck timber are spaced about 5mm ($\frac{1}{4}$") apart to allow water and dirt to flow through the deck.

The sizing of the timber and the spacing of the joists depends on the expected load and the overall size of the structure. These constructions can be designed in a variety of patterns, but each time the deck changes direction, it will need to be supported underneath. All bolts and nails should be galvanized.

Left: Timber verandahs Josiah Conder-style. Note the large stone adjacent to the verandah on which garden shoes were placed before entering the house.

Right: Construction detail of a timber verandah or decking (top) and a Conder sketch of a 'Garden of Late Springtime', showing verandahs and wisteria pergolas.

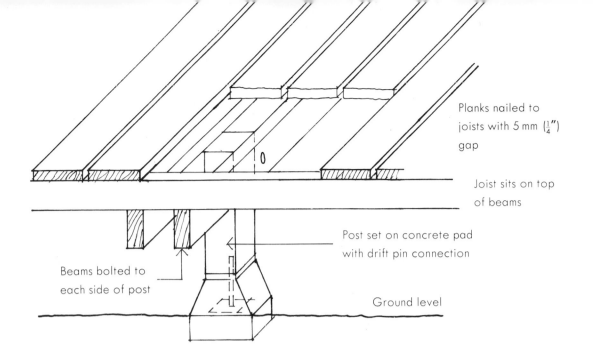

Planks nailed to
joists with 5 mm ($\frac{1}{4}$")
gap

Joist sits on top
of beams

Post set on concrete pad
with drift pin connection

Beams bolted to
each side of post

Ground level

Ornaments

The setting of ornaments, including stone lanterns, *stupas* and Buddhas, merely requires the firming of the ground before positioning the ornament upright. Tall *stupas* or towers may require more of a foundation in the form of a slab of concrete set level, but make sure that the concrete will not be visible. Rocks associated with stone lanterns are set as described earlier in the section on Rock Setting.

The setting of water basins requires only a firm foundation and care that they are set level so that the water flows over the sides equally. If the water in the basin is replenished by bucket then installation is simple. A basin filled by a stream requires you to experiment with bamboo pipes to divert the water into the basin, and needs a drain to take the water away, perhaps to form a stream again.

An alternative system is to fill the basin either by mains water or by re-cycled water from a pump. Using mains water (see below), a 15mm ($\frac{1}{2}$") pipe is led from the building's cold water system through a stop tap set in the ground in a small chamber to connect to a flexible hose. The hose is led up inside a bamboo pipe to discharge into the water basin. A simple drain to soak away would need to be provided. The water is turned on at the stop tap for the period that you want to use the basin. With this system, it is advised that a stop tap also be placed within the building and the pipe out to the basin designed so that it can be drained for the winter period in cold climates. Any local water regulations need to be satisfied.

A re-cycled water system requires the basin to sit on top of a chamber with a small submersible pump in the bottom of it. The outlet from the pump is a flexible hose that leads up through a bamboo pipe in a similar way to the previous system (see opposite). When the pump is switched on, water discharges from the bamboo pipe into the basin, overflows and drains into the chamber below, to be pumped up later to the bamboo pipe.

The pump needs to be wired up for electricity and it is best to have the switch within a building. The cable should be armoured and led through a conduit along a route that is unlikely to be disturbed. This could be alongside a wall or at about 600mm (2') depth through a shrub bed. The only drawbacks with this system are that the water in the chamber needs to be kept topped up — because if the level falls too low the pump will be damaged — and that the water should not be drunk.

A water basin filled by pipe from the water supply

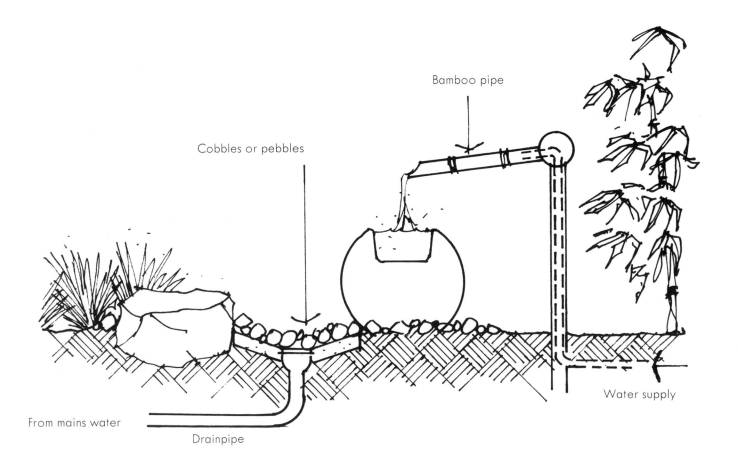

Bamboo pipe

Cobbles or pebbles

Water supply

From mains water

Drainpipe

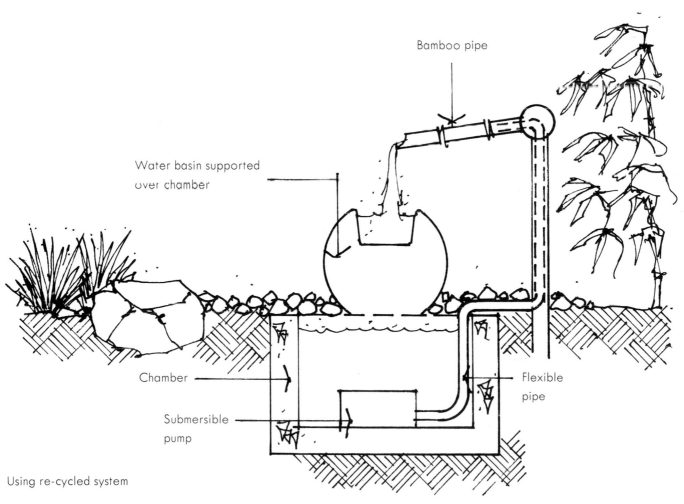

Bamboo pipe

Water basin supported over chamber

Chamber

Submersible pump

Flexible pipe

Using re-cycled system

Soil and Planting

Any soil already existing on site should be tested to find out its characteristics. This can be done either by specialist soil analysts, or by using a Do It Yourself testing kit. At the minimum you should find out the pH of the soil, that is whether it is acid or alkaline, and judge if it is loamy, clayey or sandy. Other useful tests determine the quantity of the important nutrients nitrogen, phosphorus and potassium (chemical symbols for these are N, P and K), and the organic matter content of the soil.

Plant species vary in their tolerances and preferences to soils. Some are tolerant of a range of pH and soil types whereas others are very choosy. For example, camellias,

A clipped and twisted pine, root-balled for sale in a Dutch nursery. Typically the Japanese aesthetic requires them to resemble trees grown on a windswept, rocky promontory.

rhododendrons, azaleas and *Pieris* species are not tolerant of alkaline conditions, and if you want to grow these in a basically alkaline soil then the soil surrounding them will need to be replaced with an acidic soil. Bamboos generally like a moisture-retentive soil with a reasonable clay and organic matter content, although the black bamboo (*Phyllostachys nigra*) colours up best in sandy soil.

Nutrient deficiency in soil can easily be countered by the addition of fertilizer. For small areas, slow-release fertilizers are convenient and release a range of nutrients over a period of six to twelve months.

Depth of topsoil needs to be considered. Ideally one should have a minimum of 400mm (1' 4'') on top of subsoil for shrubs, 300mm (1') for low ground covers and 150mm (6'') for grass, although plants will tolerate shallower depths. Trees require at least 600mm (2') of topsoil. These depths do not apply to roof gardens where the underlying subsoil is absent.

A list of plants suitable for a Japanese-style garden or landscape can be found at the end of the book, together with a guide to materials. Plants, with the exception of ground-covers, should be obtained as near to their mature size as possible. This means obtaining root-balled or pot-grown plants. A root-balled plant is grown in the field and then lifted together with a ball of soil, containing most of its roots, around which webbing or hessian is wrapped. A pot-grown plant is sold growing in a pot or plastic container. The other type of plant sold is 'bare-root', or 'open-ground', which is grown in the field and then lifted, so that most of the soil falls off the roots.

Trees are often sold as bare-root in Britain but usually only up to a certain size. Trees above about 4m (13' 4'') in overall height and 14 to 16cm (5½'' to 6'') stem girth (measured 1 m (3' 3'') above ground level) should be either root-balled or pot-grown. In the USA, trees are normally sold root-balled or pot-grown. Shrubs tend to be pot-grown except for some larger specimens, which can be grown in the field and root-balled.

Bare-root plants can only be planted in the winter season when the plant is dormant and, because there is the chance of the roots drying out between lifting in the field and being planted on a site, the success rate is lower. Pot-grown and root-balled plants have a higher success rate and can theoretically be planted at any time. They should not, however, be planted during hot weather, and they achieve a higher success rate if planted during the autumn, winter or spring season. Evergreens, conifers and herbaceous plants are best planted in the spring, as are bamboos, since this is when they begin to sprout.

If you have some mature plants on the site which are in the wrong position for the new design, you should consider transplanting them. Shrubs can be dug up with their root-ball without prior preparation if they are not over-large, and the best time is in the spring. Trees, however, do need preparation, ideally one or two years in advance of moving. To prepare a tree, a trench is dug at the extremity of a manageable root-ball in a circle around the trunk, and it is back-filled with some loose soil material. Any roots encountered are cut off cleanly. The trees will then put on fibrous feeding roots at the extremity of the root-ball. When the time comes to move it — and winter or spring is the best time — it is moved with the root-ball complete with covering of fibrous roots. To achieve this, the root-ball should be tied up with natural rope or strong netting, so that it can be transported intact. If you are hiring a crane to move rocks, consider using the same crane to move large trees.

To plant a tree, a pit has to be dug which, for a 3 to 5m (10' to 17') tree, should be at least 900mm (3') in diameter and 600mm (2') deep. The bottom of the pit should be loosened, the tree put in, and the hole back-filled with a mixture of soil, organic matter or compost and fertilizer, firming it as the pit is filled. Normally staking and tying with a proper tree-tie will be required. A newly planted tree should be watered regularly while it establishes itself.

The plan drawn up initially should stipulate where each plant species is to be placed, and with what amount of spacing. For a large project it is much easier to work out on a plan the numbers of plants you need to order than to try to work it out on the ground.

Spacing of the plants varies with the species, the size you are planting them at, and the desired effect. Obviously, large spreading plants and semi-mature plants which are already large are spaced well apart. However, if you are using normal nursery stock sizes in 2-, 3- or 5-litre (3½-pint, 5-pint or 1-gallon) pots, and you want the garden to look reasonably full at the start, you should plant at closer intervals and then thin out as the plants grow. Thus shrubs that will normally reach ultimate heights of 1 to 2m (3' 4'' to 7') should be planted at intervals of 500 to 750mm (1' 8'' to 2' 6''). Ground-covers should be planted between 300 and 500mm (1' to 1' 8'') apart according to their spread.

Shrubs and ground-covers are simply planted in the soil beds, but try to accommodate their preferences and tolerances for sun, shade and shelter. The tall bamboos, for instance, ideally like a south-facing slope in temperate regions, whereas shorter *Sasa* species tolerate some shade. All newly planted species should be well watered.

Maintenance

All gardens require maintenance and a Japanese one is no exception. To the untrained eye, the large areas of gravel, thickly planted ground-covers, the absence of large areas of lawn and the overall naturalism of the plants in a Japanese garden may look maintenance-free, but this is not quite true. The type of maintenance needed, however, is not laborious and should be viewed as a joy to undertake as it, too, requires a high level of sensitivity. Having created a Japanese-style garden, be sure not to hand over the maintenance to someone who has no appreciation of the art, as the garden will quickly lose all its subtleties.

The maintenance can be kept to a minimum by planting thickly and covering the ground with a layer of mulch so that weeds do not have a chance to germinate. The best mulch is natural bark and, although relatively expensive, this lasts longer than substitutes such as peat or mushroom compost. Added advantages are that its overall brown hue shows off the plants well until they spread out and cover the ground, and it helps to conserve moisture and insulates the soil below. Bamboos particularly like to be heavily mulched. Avoid bark mixed with woodchips, which is an inferior product.

Pruning is important in all gardens but, in the Japanese one, it is also a means of training plants. The Japanese mostly seek to keep their plants looking natural, but they maintain them in an artistic way to bring out certain qualities and to keep the overall form well-balanced. The two main qualities sought are age and a weather-beaten look resulting from exposure. Both of these can be achieved with time and patience by training. Pines with this gnarled, twisted, spreading form are much preferred and in Japan they can be purchased already trained. As supplies of such plant material are limited in the West, one solution is to train a young pine yourself.

To do this, you should start with a young plant not more than 1.8m (6') high which is reasonably flexible. The line drawings overleaf (left and centre) show one method where the tree is made into an S shape. It is planted at an angle in the ground, alternate branches are cut off the trunk, and the trunk is kept in the curved shape by tying it to stakes. The shape of the horizontal branches is controlled with rope or lateral poles so that they are balanced around the trunk. Where rope binds against the bark, rubber spacers should be used to reduce chafing, or else proper rubber tree-ties. Once the tree keeps its new shape, the stakes can be removed.

Other pruning is also carried out, both to the young pines being trained and also to old pines, in order to keep their appearance (as shown overleaf). A twisted appearance in a main branch is achieved by cutting part of it off just above a bud or smaller branch, so that instead of growing straight out, the branch will curve in another direction. Any straight ascending or crossing branches, which are not parallel with other horizontal ones, are also cut off. Another interesting effect is *sashide*, which involves cutting out the tip and downward-pointing small branches to give a tufted wing-like effect. As well as pine trees, maples are another favourite to be trained into a weather-beaten look.

Pruning is best carried out in late spring, and again in late summer. It achieves more than just shaping, as it allows light and air to get to the lower branches, and helps the retained branches to be vigorous. Bamboo cannot be kept in check by pruning, but dead canes should be removed. The way to halt its spread is by restricting root growth, and this can be achieved by placing concrete flags vertically just below soil level at the desired extremity of its spread and immediately cutting off shoots that appear in undesirable places.

The other maintenance tasks in the garden are watering,

fertilizing and the collection of leaves – because although Japanese gardens should look naturalistic, they should not look untidy. If you are able to water by hand regularly during the hot summer months, then simple outdoor water points or taps with a length of hose are sufficient. However, if the garden is left unattended in dry periods, an automatic irrigation system should be installed. These range from a simple time-controlled valve at a water point linked to a perforated hose, to sophisticated programmed controllers with reservoir tank and pump, linked to a system of drippers or sprays. Bamboo especially requires regular watering in the summer months.

Fertilizing can be achieved with a single application of a slow-release type containing the range of nutrients needed for healthy plant growth. One application spread in the spring is designed to release the nutrients slowly over a 6-, 9- or 12-month period. Bamboo responds to a high-nitrogen fertilizer such as well-rotted manure or compost applied in the autumn, so that it breaks down to release its nutrients for the following season.

Below: Shaping and pruning pines. Left: the trunk, bent into an 'S' shape, is tied to a stake to hold it in position. Alternate branches have been cut off. Centre: lateral poles and ropes are attached to train the horizontal branches.

Top right: vertical branches are pruned to stimulate growth of lateral branches. Trimming the tips allows more sun through to the centre of the tree. The oblique lines represent cuts. Bottom right: sashide is the method of pruning branches and twigs that project below the limb, producing a wing or feather-like shape.

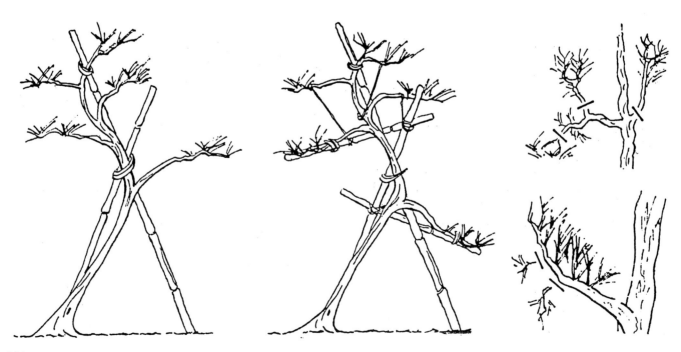

Selected Plant List

The botanical name appears first in italics. Where one exists, the common name follows in parentheses. The figures refer to the hardiness zone designations (see maps on pp. 168–9) and indicate that the plant should withstand the average *minimum* winter temperature of that zone.

Trees

Acer palmatum (Japanese maple) 6
Acer palmatum 'Heptalobum Osakazuki' 6
Betula pendula (Silver birch) 3–9
Chamaecyparis obtusa (Hinoki cypress) 5
Cryptomeria japonica (Japanese cedar) 8
Ginkgo biloba (Maidenhair tree) Hardy through zone 5
Pinus contorta (Beach pine) 4
Pinus densiflora (Japanese red pine) 5, but sometimes damaged in severe winters
Pinus parviflora (Japanese white pine) 6
Pinus sylvestris (Scots pine) 3
Pinus thunbergii (Japanese black pine) 5
Prunus mume (Japanese apricot) 7
Prunus subhirtella 'Pendula' (Weeping Higan cherry) 6
Prunus x yedoensis (Yoshino cherry) 6
Sorbus aucuparia (Mountain ash) 2
Thuja plicata (Western red cedar) 5, but needs protection

Large shrubs

Aucuba japonica (Spotted laurel) 8
Camellia japonica (Common camellia) 8
Camellia japonica 'Hortensis' 8
Choisya ternata (Mexican orange blossom) 8
Euonymus japonicus 8
Fatsia japonica (False castor oil plant) 8
Hamamelis japonica (Japanese witch hazel) 5
Ligustrum japonicum (Japanese privet) 8
Osmanthus fragrans 8
Photinia x fraseri 'Red Robin' 8
Pieris japonica 7
Pinus densiflora 'Umbraculifera' (Tanyosho pine) 6, sometimes damaged in severe winters
Pinus mugo (Mountain pine) 3
Pittosporum tobira 8
Podocarpus macrophylla 8
Punica granatum (Pomegranate) 9

Medium shrubs

Berberis thunbergii (Barberry) 4—8

Buxus microphylla (Small-leaved box) 6

Chaenomeles speciosa (C. lagenaria) (Japanese quince) 5

Hypericum x moserianum (Form of St John's wort) 6

Ilex crenata (Holly) 6

Mahonia japonica 6

Nandina doméstica (Sacred bamboo) 7, attains full growth
only in zone 7, but is root-hardy in zone 6 in protected
places

Olearia x haastii (Daisy bush) 8

Rhododendron species (Species of azalea) 4—8, depending
on particular species

Rhododendron obtusum (Kirishima azalea) 7

Low shrubs/ground cover/herbaceous

Arenaria species (Form of sandwort) 3—4

Aspidistra elatior 8

Cotoneaster dammeri 6

Erica carnea 6

Eurya japonica Greenhouse culture or outside in moist, half-
shady sites in zone 9

Festuca orina Var. glauca 4

Helixine soleirolii (Baby's tears) 4

Hosta species (Plantain lily) 4

Iris foetidissima (Stinking iris) 7

Iris japonica 8

Iris kaempferi 5

Juniperus horizontalis (Creeping juniper) 3

Liriope muscari 6

Ophiopogon japonicus 7

Pachysandra terminalis 5

Phragmites species (Reed) 6

Polystichum aculeatum (Hard shield fern) 6

Polytrichum commune ('Haircap' moss) 7, 8

Saxifraga stolonifera (Species of saxifrage) 7

Thymus serpyllum (Wild thyme) 4

Vaccinium vitis-idaea (Cowberry) 6

Vinca minor (Lesser periwinkle) 5

Zoysia tenuifolia 10

Climbers

Clematis patens (Clematis) 5

Parthenocissus tricuspidata (Boston ivy) 5

Wisteria floribunda (Japanese wisteria) 5

Bamboos and palms

Arundinaria pumila 8

Arundinaria viridistriata (A. auricoma) 8

Cycas revoluta 9

Phyllostachys aurea (Golden bamboo) 8

Phyllostachys nigra (Black bamboo) 8

Phyllostachys nigra Var. henonis (Henon bamboo) 8

Sasa palmata 7

Sasa veitchii 8

Thamnocalanus spathaceus (Arundinaria murieliae) 8

Trachycarpus fortunei (Chamaerops excelsa) (Chusan, or
windmill palm) 9

Hardiness Zones

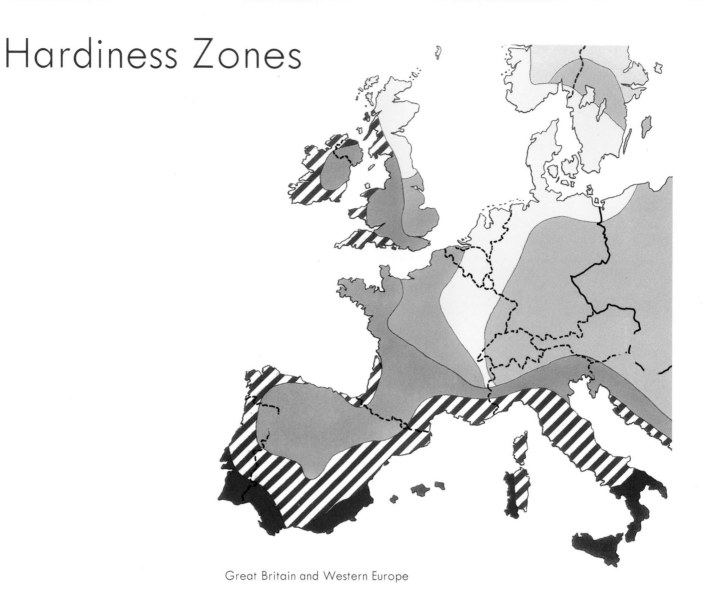

Great Britain and Western Europe

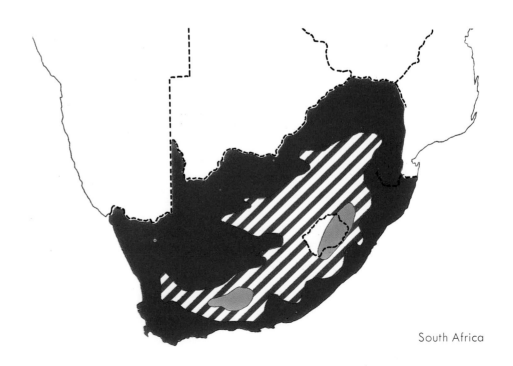

South Africa

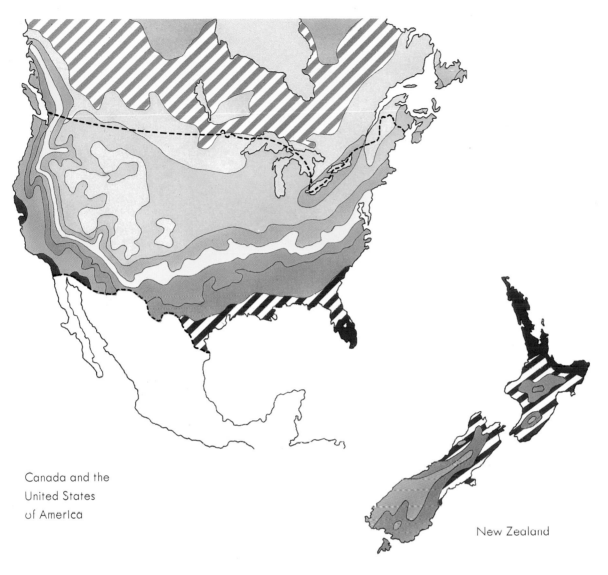

Canada and the
United States
of America

New Zealand

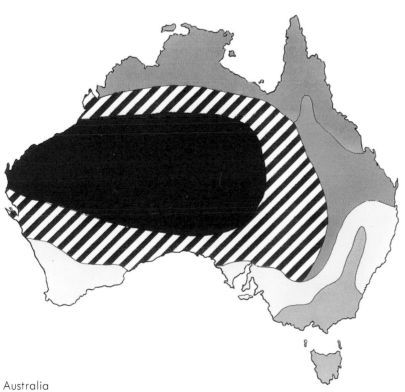

Australia

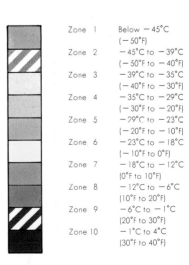

	Zone 1	Below −45°C (−50°F)
	Zone 2	−45°C to −39°C (−50°F to −40°F)
	Zone 3	−39°C to −35°C (−40°F to −30°F)
	Zone 4	−35°C to −29°C (−30°F to −20°F)
	Zone 5	−29°C to −23°C (−20°F to −10°F)
	Zone 6	−23°C to −18°C (−10°F to 0°F)
	Zone 7	−18°C to −12°C (0°F to 10°F)
	Zone 8	−12°C to −6°C (10°F to 20°F)
	Zone 9	−6°C to −1°C (20°F to 30°F)
	Zone 10	−1°C to 4°C (30°F to 40°F)

Guide to Materials

Hard Materials

As materials in Japanese gardens are almost exclusively natural, what is available for use depends on your locality. Heavy materials extracted locally will be more readily available and also cheaper, for haulage is a significant cost factor. Do not, however, be tempted to compromise a design by using materials that are not exactly right.

Rocks and loose materials (such as gravel and cobbles) can be obtained from stone companies, some nurseries and garden centres. Loose materials are also available from some well-stocked builders' merchants. As rock types vary in size, shape and colour of material, they need to be individually selected. Gravel and cobbles vary in colour, size and shape, according to where they were extracted, and it is essential to obtain samples before ordering a large quantity.

Stone ornaments, such as lanterns, water basins and *stupas*, are available in reconstituted stone from some nurseries, garden centres and specialist companies. Real stone ones are imported from the Far East, but only in limited numbers.

The timber that is available also varies according to your locality. Hardwoods are naturally resistant to rot, but softwoods need to be treated against rot, and the best method for this is vacuum-pressure impregnation. The wood can be coloured by applying a decorative timber treatment, which is designed to stay in the wood for several years. Avoid using stains, as these are easily washed out. Whatever treatment you choose, check that it is not harmful to fish or plants.

In some areas it can be difficult to find bamboo suitable for use in construction, but a few nurseries and garden centres do stock it. To buy bamboo fences and gates you will need to find someone who imports them from the Far East.

Plant Materials

The Selected Plant List contains both plants that the Japanese would use in a traditional garden and others more common in the West, which may be used while still following the spirit of such gardens. The list is not intended to be exhaustive, but to inspire you to search out species with useful characteristics that grow well in your locality; for example, try using low ground-covers as a substitute for moss, if your climate is not conducive to moss growth.

Where the species has both a Common and a Botanical name, both are given. When ordering plants you should always use the Botanical name, as the Common name can vary with country and locality and you could easily end up with the wrong plant. For the characteristics of each species, their preferences, their tolerances and their mature size, you should consult other reference material.

The availability of plants also varies with country and locality, but a comprehensive nursery or garden centre should either stock what you are looking for or be able to order it for you. It can be difficult to find plants of the size and shape you want: large specimens are often particularly hard to find, and trees or plants that have been trained into shapes are even more scarce.

Trees and plants may be sold bare-root, root-balled or pot-grown (these terms are explained in Chapter 5). In the USA, most plants are sold root-balled or pot-grown. In Britain, shrubs and ground-covers are also usually sold in this state, but trees are often sold bare-root.

Trees in Britain are graded according to the girth (circumference) of the trunk, measured 1m (3' 3") above ground level. In the USA, trees are graded according to the calliper (diameter) of the trunk, measured 150mm (6") above ground level up to 100mm (4") calliper, and 300mm (12") above ground level for larger sizes. Shrubs and ground-covers are graded according to their height, spread and pot size. The most important factor when choosing trees for a Japanese garden, however, is whether their overall shape suits their position in the design.

Having gained the knowledge,
now is the time to create.

Below: Picture windows from conference rooms open on to this garden for an office atrium, where a water course, beginning as a spring bubbler, falls over waterfalls and into a cobble-edged pond. A bamboo grove enhances the tranquil atmosphere. (Designer: Philip Cave Associates)

A dry landscape garden created in a narrow outdoor space behind London's Strand. A stream, symbolized by pebbles, meanders between large boulders with a backdrop of bamboo and camellias and a moss-like ground cover.

Index

Acknowledgements

It is always a joy to reflect on those people who have assisted you in such a quest for knowledge and design technique. However, it is difficult to know how far back to go — where, for instance, was that initial spark of interest created, and which peripheral encounters affected later ideas?

Concentrating on the immediate past, my *sensei*, or master, Professor Kinsaku Nakane from Kyoto, should be thanked for willingly imparting his knowledge and for allowing me to work with him and his son, Shiro. Ken Nakajima and his sons were also very helpful, as was Haruto Kobayashi from Tokyo, who gave support and guidance. As Japanese gardens are so interrelated with the deeper workings of the mind, I am indebted to those people who have been my teachers in this field, especially Swami Shyam. I would like to mention those people who made reference material available — particularly the Landscape Institute Library, and Sir Geoffrey Jellicoe, who has in addition inspired me through his writings, talks and now his Foreword. Both Steven Morrell of the John P. Humes Japanese Stroll Garden and Graham Holloway were also helpful in commenting on the plant list and its relevance to the USA. Finally my gratitude goes to Annie for her support and constructive critiques.

Bibliography

Bring, Mitchell, and Wayemberghe, Josse, *Japanese Gardens, Design and Meaning* (McGraw-Hill, 1981)

Conder, Josiah, *Landscape Gardening in Japan* (1893; Dover reprint, 1963)

Davidson, A.K., *Zen Gardening* (Rider and Company, 1982)

Engel, David, *Japanese Gardens for Today* (Tuttle, 1959)

Hayakawa, Masao, *The Garden Art of Japan* (Weatherhill, 1973)

Higuchi, Tadahiko, *The Visual Art and Spatial Structure of Landscapes* (MIT, 1983)

Iguchi, Kaisen, *Tea Ceremony* (Hoikusha, 1975)

Itoh, Teiji, *The Japanese Garden* (Yale, 1972)

— *Space and Illusion in the Japanese Garden* (Weatherhill/Tankosha, 1973)

Kuck, Loraine, *The World of the Japanese Garden* (Weatherhill, 1968)

Nakane, Kinsaku, *Kyoto Gardens* (Hoikusha, 1965)

Seike, Kiyoshi, Kudo, Masanobu and Engel, David H., *A Japanese Touch for your Garden* (Kodansha International, 1980)

Shimoyama, Shigemaru, translator of *Sakuteiki: The Book of Garden* by Toshitsuna Tachibana (Town and City Planners, 1976)

Picture Credits

The author and publishers are grateful to the following for permission to reproduce illustrations:

Heather Angel: p.*60*
Aspect Picture Library/Bill Tingey: p.*79*
Peter Baistow: p.*104*
Ian Bott: plans on pp.*37, 41, 64*
Bridgeman Art Library/Tokyo National Museum: p.*20*
Camera Press/William MacQuitty: p.*52–3*
Philip Cave: pp.*21* (bottom), *33, 34, 35, 36, 45, 55* (top), *56, 58* (both), *61, 75, 78* (left), *84, 92, 99, 101, 108, 126, 142* (left), *148, 149, 151, 161* (top), *162, 172, 173*
Philip Cave Associates: pp.*134, 137* (right), *140–1, 184*
Graham Challifour: pp.*94–5*
Joy FitzSimmons: line illustrations on pp.*92–3, 96, 99, 102–3, 110–11, 114–15, 119, 122–3, 124–5, 153*
Fushin-an, Omote Senke: p.*57*
Garden Picture Library/Rex Butcher: pp.*59, 73, 87* (left)
Hutchinson Picture Library: pp.*26–7*
Imperial Household Agency: pp.*2–3*
Japanese Cultural Centre: p.*109*

Professor Kinsaku Nakane: pp.*21, 139, 152*
Kirk Nelson: construction drawings on pp.*137* (left), *138, 142* (right), *145, 146, 147, 149, 150, 151, 155, 159* (top), *160, 161* (bottom)
Oxford Scientific Films/Deni Bown: pp.*70–1*
Bill Tingey: pp.*12–13, 14–15, 16, 17, 18–19, 30* (both), *31, 39, 40, 42, 43, 44, 48, 50, 51, 54–5, 62–3* (both), *65, 67, 74, 76–7, 78* (right), *81, 82–3, 85, 86, 87* (right), *90–1, 97, 98, 105, 106, 107, 113, 115, 116* (both), *117* (both), *119* (bottom), *122* (top), *123* (top), *124* (top), *125* (top), *127, 128* (both), *156, 157, 165*
Tokyo National Museum: p.*47*
Hugh Williams: maps on pp.*168–9*
Yukki Yaura: calligraphy on pp.*10, 24, 68, 88, 132*

Gardens depicted on the following pages were designed by Philip Cave Associates: pp.*75, 134, 137* (right), *140–1, 148, 151, 161, 172, 173*